LIGHTS UP

A COLLECTION OF 20 RIDICULOUS SCENES FOR YOUNG ACTORS

WRITTEN BY JOSHUA EVANS
ILLUSTRATED BY SEAN HALL

COPYRIGHT © 2019 JOSHUA EVANS
ALL RIGHTS RESERVED.

SOME THOUGHTS ON THESE SILLY SCRIBBLINGS

"Write Characters... and have fun."

I began working and writing for children's theatre programs in Los Angeles back in 2004. Writing for kids can be tricky, and as any writer can attest, staring at a blank page on your computer screen can be quite terrifying. You're constantly wrestling with your battle-worn enemies, Doubt and Uncertainty. I would repeatedly have a flash of a brilliant idea, only to have it shot down and destroyed by these two foes. Over the years I eventually found a useful tool in my literary war with Doubt and Uncertainty: Characters. Focus On The Characters. With this as my battle-cry, I had the privilege and joy of writing and staging over 75 of these children's theatre scenes.

So now, every time I'm staring down a blank page ready to do battle, I have the same goal rattling around in my head, "Write Characters... and have fun."

It's my firm belief that young actors are much more interested in playing bold characters, rather than getting bogged down in heavy plot. Professional theatre educators (far more trained than me!) may differ, but I found time and time again that the scenes I wrote with strong *characters,* rather than complicated or clever *plot*, were much, much more popular with the kids. They want Characters!

Go ahead and ask them. Young actors are dying to play strong Characters! I believe that it's one of the main reasons why they're experimenting with theatre at this time in their lives: to be someone(thing?) completely different from what they are in real life. So let them! Encourage them to play! Let's give them far-out characters to perform. Let's see them be the hungry cannibal, the saucy hologram, the dumb caveman, the angry genie, or the time-traveling high schooler!

There are shelves and shelves of scene books for young actors that bring so much real life doom and gloom to the stage. I've read so many scenes and monologues that have young actors dive deep into tough subjects like death, loneliness, divorce, bullying, or worse. There's definitely a time and place for these... but where are all the fun scenes?! These silly scribblings provide that: Fun.

I truly believe that the average young actor is more interested in being in a fun scene, as opposed to a serious, deeply emotional one. And that was the other half of my often repeated thought: give them something to have *fun* with! There's plenty of time in their acting career to explore deep, dark, terrifying emotions. But right now, why not have fun? Give them the joy of making the audience fall in love with their silliness.

Tell them: Go!
Have a blast!
Be that awesome character!
Make that audience laugh!
The stage is lit, and is eagerly waiting for your creativity and joy!
Go. Have. Fun.

-Joshua Evans, 2019

For my Family,
Stephanie and Archer

~

Special Thanks to all those
amazing, energetic, crazy, and talented kids
who originally brought these Silly Scribblings to life

Tonight's Scenes

Philophobia
~ 2 ~

Ryan's Fans
~ 10 ~

The Garden
~ 16 ~

Marion vs. Marion
~ 26 ~

So You Think You Can News
~ 32 ~

Trapped
~ 42 ~

Kitchen Floor
~ 48 ~

Atlantis!
~ 56 ~

Sandwich
~ 62 ~

Isla Peligroso – 1839
~ 68 ~

A Saturday Afternoon
~ 76 ~

Totally
~ 84 ~

Mysterious Mysteries
~ 90 ~

Smiling Unicorn
~ 98 ~

Survival: Danger Island [2039]
~ 106 ~

Cannon and Radford
~ 114 ~

Time Reporting
~ 120 ~

The Commodore and The Admiral
~ 130 ~

Final Exam
~ 138 ~

Cindy's Best Day Ever
~ 146 ~

A Quick Note Regarding Character Gender

Who cares?!

These scenes were all written for crazy theatre programs with fluctuating enrollment, so I had to change genders of the characters *all the time.* Young actors can get so hung up on whether their character is a "girl or a boy", but I say it doesn't matter! Every single one of these scenes has been performed with some variation of gender swapping.

Why not give the young actor the choice? That's what I always did. I told them, "Look, I know the character is written as a boy, but I'm going to leave it up to you. Do you want to play it as a girl instead? Do you want to keep it a boy? Do you even care? Do you want me to change the name to make you more comfortable? Tell me what you want to do."

You'd be surprised how many times the young actor will actually be interested in playing an opposite gender!

Hey... it worked for Shakespeare!

LIGHTS UP

"You've never been on this ride? Oh, you're gonna get so spooked!"

Philophobia

(Lights up as STEVE and JENNY are being pushed on stage in their boat)

JENNY: Ooooooooo... how romantic, Stevie. The Tunnel of Love.

STEVE: What? This? No, this isn't the Tunnel of Love.

JENNY: But the sign outside said, "Tunnel of Love".

STEVE: No, it said "Tunnel of *the Fear* of Love". Yeah, it's a *scary* ride.

JENNY: It didn't say that. That's ridiculous. Besides, how can you be afraid of falling in love?

STEVE: "All the frightening stages of falling in love, played out in escalating phobias."

JENNY: Falling in love isn't supposed to be frightening.

STEVE: You've never been on this ride? Oh, you're gonna get so

Philophobia

spooked!

> *(They come to their first vignette, a BOYFRIEND and a GIRLFRIEND are frozen until they arrive)*

BOYFRIEND: What so you mean I can't go to the game this weekend?

STEVE: Oh oh oh! Fear of Commitment. This one's terrifying!

GIRLFRIEND: You can't go to the game this weekend, cuz we're going to Ikea for a picture frame.

BOYFRIEND: I don't need a picture frame.

GIRLFRIEND: If we're gonna put up a picture of us in your apartment, then we need a frame.

BOYFRIEND: A picture of us? Whoa! This is moving pretty fast.

GIRLFRIEND: This is moving pretty fast? We've been dating for over a year... *(Grabs a pillow and starts beating him with it)* Who is she?!! What's her name?!! You hanging out with some other girl?!!

BOYFRIEND: Ow! Stop! She and I are just friends! We work together! Ow! Let's not put labels on things!

> *(The BOYFRIEND and GIRLFRIEND freeze, as the boat moves on)*

JENNY: Are you kidding me?

STEVE: Phew! That was pretty scary.

JENNY: As a woman, I found that pretty derogatory!

STEVE: No, that dude just wanted his space.

Philophobia *Joshua Evans*

JENNY: After dating for over a year?! And he admitted that he had some girl on the side.

STEVE: Shhhh! Here comes the next one!

(They come to their second vignette. The same actors from the first vignette are now COOPER and MOM. They are frozen until the boat arrives)

COOPER: It's nice to finally meet you, Mrs. Anderson.

JENNY: Lemme guess: fear of meeting the parents?

STEVE: Soceraphobia!

MOM: Well, well, well, we finally get to meet the infamous Cooper.

COOPER: That's me!

MOM: Tell me a bit about yourself.

COOPER: Not much to tell.

MOM: I'm sure.

JENNY: Burn!

MOM: Job?

COOPER: No.

MOM: Car?

COOPER: Nuh-uh.

MOM: Apartment?

Philophobia

COOPER: Parent's basement.

MOM: Diplomas?

COOPER: Nadas.

MOM: And what makes you think you're good enough to date my daughter?

COOPER: Um... I play guitar, and I have a sweet van?

MOM: Time to go.

(COOPER and MOM freeze, as the boat moves on)

STEVE: Man! That Mom was vicious!

JENNY: Are you kidding me? That boyfriend was a loser! She was protecting her daughter.

STEVE: Why are parents always so mean?

JENNY: Are you not paying attention at all?!

STEVE: Oh no! The scariest one yet! Philophobia!!

JENNY: What's that?

STEVE: *(Covers his eyes)* I can't watch!

(They come to their third vignette, with the same vignette actors again, this time as KYLE and ARIA. They are frozen until the boat arrives)

ARIA: Kyle?

Philophobia

KYLE: Yeah, Babe?

ARIA: Kyle, put down the controller.

KYLE: *(Puts down controller)* What is it, Babe?

ARIA: We've been together for two and a half years now, and I need to tell you something.

KYLE: Hit me, Babe.

ARIA: Kyle... I love you.

KYLE: Ooooohhh... thank you. *(Picks up controller again)*

ARIA: Um... don't you have anything *else* to say to me?

KYLE: Oh! Thank you ***very much.***

ARIA: Annnnd?

KYLE: Annnnd... you rock.

ARIA: Kyle!

KYLE: Babe?

ARIA: I love you!

KYLE: Awesome.

ARIA: I love you!

KYLE: You're the best.

ARIA: I love you!

Philophobia

KYLE: RightBackAtchya

ARIA: Last chance, Kyle! I love you!

KYLE: *(Raises his hand)* High-five.

(ARIA lets out a frustrated grunt, and they both freeze. The boat slowly moves away)

JENNY: Let me guess... the fear of saying "I love you".

STEVE: Whoa! Careful with that phrase! Don't just go swinging it around like that.

JENNY: How long have we been together, Stevie?

STEVE: I dunno... at least three NFL seasons now.

JENNY: Steve, I love you.

(There is a long stand-off as STEVE is struggling to find the right words, and JENNY repeatedly stops him from saying anything except "I love you". No words are spoken though. STEVE runs out of things to try to say, and simply raises his hand)

STEVE: High-five?

JENNY: We're through, Steven!

(And with that, JENNY storms off the boat, and exits, leaving STEVE alone. Just then, another boat comes along)

AARON: *(Looking at STEVE)* Oooo! They added a new one onto this ride!

DEBBIE: Monophobia...

Philophobia Joshua Evans

AARON: The fear of being alone. How pathetic.

DEBBIE: *(Raises her hand for a high-five)* I love you!

AARON: *(High-fives her)* I love you!

BLACKOUT

*"Whatever! Shall we tell the **real** story behind your 'signed headshot'?"*

Ryan's Fans

(KELLY, STACEY, and JENNY enter. They settle themselves, look at each other, and let out a scream of happiness and anticipation)

KELLY: *(Settling)* Oh my gawsh! I can't believe that we are about to see **the** Ryan Fresh.

STACEY: After a show like that? He is *so* talented.

JENNY: He is the best stage actor of our time.

KELLY: The **best**.

STACEY: Are you sure that he will come this way?

JENNY: Of course I'm sure. My friend works backstage, and she tells me that he *always* comes out of this door.

KELLY: We'll have the **perfect** view of him.

STACEY: I'm sooooo excited!

Ryan's Fans

(All three girls hug each other, jump up and down, and scream)

JENNY: *(Settling)* Aren't you ladies glad that I told you about him?

KELLY: Actually, I had already read about him.

STACEY: But I was the first to hear him sing.

JENNY: After I had seen him act.

KELLY: But only after I had seen him dance.

STACEY: And he is soooooo hot!

(All three girls hug each other, jump up and down, and scream)

JENNY: This is almost as good as when I saw him in Seattle.

KELLY: It can't be nearly as fantastic as when I accidentally ran into him in Chicago.

STACEY: Please. Those pale in comparison to when I was standing in line with him at Starbucks in New York. I was so embarrassed to realize that I had forgotten my wallet, and he totally bought my coffee for me.

KELLY: Whatever. You were *totally* stalking him.

STACEY: Was not!

KELLY: Were too!

STACEY: Why would you say such a horrible thing?

KELLY: Hmmmmm… let's think. Oh. How about when you texted me and said, "I'm totally stalking Ryan Fresh right now. I'm gonna

Ryan's Fans   *Joshua Evans*

pretend that I forgot my wallet, so I'll have an excuse to talk to him."

JENNY: That's pretty pathetic.

STACEY: Whatever! Shall we tell the *real* story behind your "signed headshot"?

JENNY: What? In Seattle, he signed one of his headshots for me.

STACEY: Stealing a signed credit card receipt out of the trash and stapling it to his headshot does not count as a signed headshot.

KELLY: You guys are sad. At least I have one of his trademark sweatbands: signed *and* sweated in.

JENNY: Which you *stole* out of his gym locker in Hawaii!

KELLY: It's still his, and it's still signed.

JENNY: "Nike" is not his Hawaiian name! I don't care what you say.

KELLY: *(Pointing at STACEY)* Well, she stole his mail.

STACEY: *(Pointing at JENNY)* She stole his wallet.

JENNY: *(Pointing at KELLY)* She stole his car.

(On the verge of a serious altercation, the three girls stand frozen with their accusatory fingers still pointed at one another. They finally slip into a silly giggle at each other)

KELLY: Remember the group photo of the four of us in LA?

STACEY: When we snuck into his dressing room while he was napping?

Ryan's Fans

JENNY: It's my screen saver at work.

KELLY: Mine too!

STACEY: Because he is so hot!

(All three girls hug each other, jump up and down, and scream)

JENNY: Oh my gawsh. Here he comes!

(RYAN FRESH comes strutting out. As he walks away, the girls scream and holler to get his attention. Eventually, he turns around and blows the girls a kiss. The girls each reach up to catch the kiss as if they were the intended mark. RYAN FRESH exits. The girls bring their enclosed fists to their chest, and let out a huge lovesick sigh. At this sound, the girls looks at each other)

STACEY, JENNY, KELLY: That was *so* meant for me!

BLACKOUT

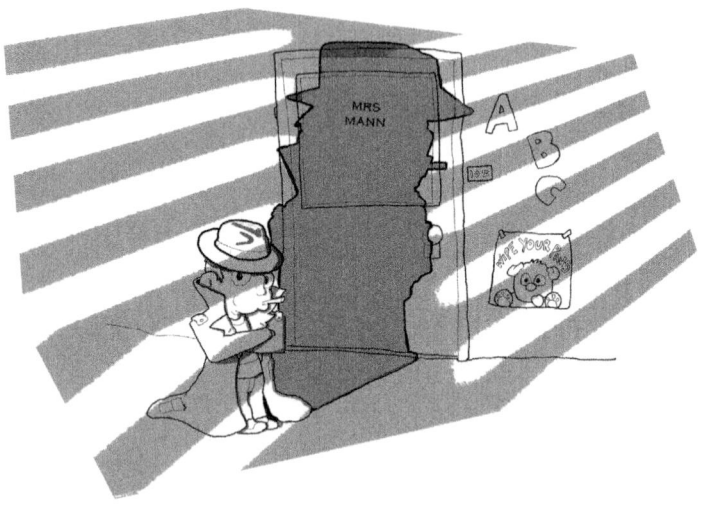

"Nap Time. And it was a hot one. The kind where your blanky stuck to you. It had been a rough couple of naps here in Mrs. Mann's kindergarten class, or as it was called on the streets, The Garden."

THE GARDEN

(Lights up on a kindergarten room. All the students are lying on their mats, blankets pulled over them, ready for nap time. MRS. MANN, the kindergarten teacher, is exiting the room)

MRS. MANN: Alright boys and girls, it's Nap Time. I want everyone to be well rested for the rest of our kindergarten day. Sleep tight, boys and girls.

ALL: Sleep tight, Mrs. Mann.

(MRS. MANN turns off the lights and exits. Dramatic Lighting and Classic Film Noir music plays, as VINNIE sits up. He's dressed in a trenchcoat, and pulls out a fedora to wear)

VINNIE: Nap Time. And it was a hot one. The kind where your blanky stuck to you. It had been a rough couple of naps here in Mrs. Mann's kindergarten class, or as it was called on the streets, The Garden. I couldn't sleep anymore, so I decided to wake up.

(JOEY wakes up. He too is wearing a trenchcoat and fedora)

The Garden

JOEY: Vinnie? What are you doing?

VINNIE: I'm being your voiceover.

JOEY: Why?

VINNIE: Cuz every good detective needs a cool voiceover.

JOEY: Oh. Ok.

VINNIE: I hadn't worked in a while, and I needed a job... soon.

(LILLY wakes up. She's wearing a long, red nightgown or dress)

VINNIE: But when I saw her, I knew this job was gonna be trouble.

LILLY: Joey, I need your help.

VINNE: She was trouble, with a capital "T". She smelled like perfume and playdough... a deadly combination.

JOEY: What can I do for you, Doll?

LILLY: My mommy packed a special cupcake in my lunch and now it's gone.

JOEY: And you want me to find it?

LILLY: I'll make it worth your while... we could split it.

VINNIE: I knew she was playing me, but I couldn't resist those puppy dog eyes.

JOEY: *(To VINNIE)* Yes I can!

VINNIE: No, you couldn't.

The Garden *Joshua Evans*

JOEY: Fine. I'll help you, Lilly.

VINNIE: Like I said, I needed the work.

JOEY: Let's go check out Tony's place.

(They start to make their way towards TONY)

VINNIE: Tony the Treat. He'd gotten involved with birthday snacks awhile back, and since then nothing came in or out of The Garden without his say-so.

LILLY: You think Tony the Treat has something to do with my missing cupcake?

JOEY: Maybe.

LILLY: Ew... The Cubby District. I hate going into his part of The Garden.

(MUTT wakes up. She's dressed in a dirty tank top. She stops the group)

MUTT: Whoa! What you guys want?

JOEY: Hey Mutt, how's it going?

VINNIE: Ugh. Mutt. Tony the Treat's muscle. Only thing worse than her name was her intelligence.

MUTT: Mutt hear you, Vinnie.

JOEY: Nevermind him. We're here to see Tony.

MUTT: Tony sleep now. Come back during Story Time.

The Garden

LILLY: We want to see him right now.

MUTT: Mutt said come back later.

LILLY: You meanie, just let us see him!

VINNIE: This dame was gonna get me a hospital bill.

MUTT: You keep girl quiet, Joey!

> *(JOEY pulls out a squeeky toy and offers it to MUTT)*

JOEY: Mutt, you let us see Tony, and I'll give you this toy...

MUTT: Squeeky!

> *(MUTT takes the toy, and wakes up TONY. He's dressed in a derby hat and suspenders)*

TONY: Mutt! I told you not to wake me unless that shipment of birthday doughnuts came in!

MUTT: Sorry boss, but look who's here.

TONY: Aaahh... Joey and Lilly. What brings you to this neck of The Garden? Lilly, I thought you were too good for the Cubby District.

LILLY: Your mat smells like the Lost and Found.

TONY: Charming as ever, Lilly.

JOEY: Tony, we don't want no trouble. We're just looking for Lilly's special cupcake.

TONY: So... Precious lost her cupcake, and you think I had something to do with it?

The Garden *Joshua Evans*

VINNIE: He was playing with us. He knew something.

TONY: What's he doing?

JOEY: He thinks he's my voiceover.

TONY: Voiceover? Why?

LILLY: It's kinda cute.

MUTT: Mutt wishes Mutt had voiceover.

TONY: Does he ever talk directly to you?

JOEY: No, it's mostly just to himself.

TONY: Really?

JOEY: Yeah.

TONY: Huh.

(They all look at VINNIE)

VINNIE: The tension was boiling hot!

LILLY: Where's my cupcake?!

TONY: Show some respect!

JOEY: Lay off her, Tony!

MUTT: Squeeky!

TONY: Look, I don't know nothing about your cupcake. You gotta go deeper.

The Garden

JOEY: Katie?

TONY: Katie.

VINNIE: I was hoping it wouldn't come to this. The last thing I wanted to do was disturb Katie the Kingpin.

JOEY: Thanks Tony. Wanna play four square at recess?

TONY: Cool!

(JOEY, LILLY, and VINNIE make their way towards KATIE)

VINNIE: Katie the Kingpin. This was bigger than I thought. We were gonna have to play this cool.

(They stand above a sleeping KATIE)

KATIE: *(Eyes still closed)* I don't have your stupid cupcake.

VINNIE: She wasn't asleep! She got the drop on us!

JOEY: Come on, Katie, cop to it. We know you got it.

LILLY: Yeah, there ain't nobody else left.

KATIE: *(Opens her eyes and sits up. She's dressed in a flowing white nightgown)* Why would I want your silly cupcake, Lilly?

LILLY: Because you were always jealous of my mommy's peanut butter cupcakes!

KATIE: Your mommy's peanut butter cupcakes?

(KATIE begins to chuckle, and works herself into a full-on laughing fit)

The Garden Joshua Evans

KATIE: Oh, my dear Joseph, you're in over your head. Go back to your mat, and sleep this one off.

VINNIE: What was she talking about?

JOEY: Yeah, what are you talking about?

KATIE: This one's too big, even for you, Joseph. Go back to your corner and pretend this never happened.

(JOEY pulls out a squirt gun, and aims it at KATIE)

JOEY: Not this time, Katie. You're gonna tell us everything!

KATIE: A squirt gun? You can do better than that, Joey.

JOEY: It's filled with grape juice. And that's an expensive looking gown.

KATIE: You wouldn't dare.

JOEY: Tell me where the cupcake is!

KATIE: It's gone. And it ain't never coming back!

JOEY: Spill the beans, or I spill the juice!

KATIE: For the last time, Joseph: walk away!

(MRS. MANN enters, and turns on the lights)

MRS. MANN: Joey! Put that down. What are you doing?

VINNIE: Oh no! It's The Mann.

LILLY: Mrs. Mann, Katie took my peanut butter cupcake!

The Garden

KATIE: Did not!

MRS. MANN: Girls, stop yelling. I took the cupcake.

JOEY: What?

MRS. MANN: Mutt has an extreme peanut allergy, and we can't have you bringing in peanut butter.

MUTT: Mutt very sensitive.

VINNIE: The whole time, it was the Mann.

MRS. MANN: All of you, go back to your mats. Because of this, I'm adding an extra fifteen minutes to Nap Time. Now, sleep tight!

(All the children make their way back to their mats and lie down. MRS. MANN storms out of the room, turning the lights off again. The music and lighting returns)

VINNIE: Yup, life's pretty tough here in The Garden. Even The Mann is out to take what she wants from ya. Lilly never got her cupcake, and I never got paid. But what do you expect? Just another lousy Nap Time here in... The Garden.

BLACKOUT

"Listen Honey, this production ain't gonna be big enough for the two of us."

Marion vs. Marion

(EMILY walks on stage with her backpack. Smiles. KELSEY walks on stage with her backpack. Smiles. Both girls see each other. Their smiles disappear, and a squinty-eyed showdown looms)

EMILY: You.

KELSEY: You.

EMILY: Trying out for Little John, then?

KELSEY: Ha, ha, ha… I didn't know they held auditions for the spotlight operator.

EMILY: Cute.

KELSEY: I know.

EMILY: Listen, Sweetheart, when they put up the casting notice for Maid Marion…

KELSEY: You can read?

Marion vs. Marion

EMILY: *(Pause)* They were looking for someone who can handle a lead role.

KELSEY: *(Referring to herself)* Like Annie, Snow White, Juliet…

EMILY: …and Chorus Girl #8.

KELSEY: That was a fluke! I auditioned with Mono!

EMILY: And you performed like it too.

KELSEY: Why you…

EMILY: Yes, good question: Why me? Perhaps they recognized the depth that I brought to such roles as Wendy, Anne Frank, Jasmine…

KELSEY: You **did** bring them to a new low.

EMILY: Spotlight Chaser!

KELSEY: One Character Wonder!

(PROCTOR enters)

PROCTOR: Welcome everyone to the auditions for Robin Hood. We are about to get started, so please be patient with us. We'll be calling you in very soon.

KELSEY: Listen Honey, this production ain't gonna be big enough for the two of us.

EMILY: My thoughts exactly.

KELSEY: So why not take it easy on yourself?

EMILY: I thought I had, by placing my name on the cast sheet… oh,

Marion vs. Marion   *Joshua Evans*

I mean the audition sheet.

KELSEY: What makes you think you have a chance against me?

EMILY: Um… I've seen you act.

KELSEY: Like when I spent two hours crying with you in the girl's restroom when Andy dumped you?

(Both girls stop. Their snippy personas drop)

EMILY: *(Genuinely hurt)* Hey...

KELSEY: *(Knows she's gone too far, and she's sorry)* Too low?

EMILY: *(Hurt)* A little bit.

KELSEY: Sorry.

EMILY: He was a jerk to me.

KELSEY: He really was. I know. I'm sorry.

EMILY: It's okay. Let's just keep this professional, okay?

KELSEY: Professional, agreed.

(Both girls instantly snap back into their cat-fight attitude)

EMILY: You have no chance!

KELSEY: In your dreams! That role is *so* mine.

EMILY: But I absolutely must have *this* role.

KELSEY: I will be destroyed if I do not get *this* role.

Marion vs. Marion

EMILY: "Maid Marion" is the only thing in the world for me!

KELSEY: "Maid Marion" is the only thing in the universe for me!

EMILY: "Maid Marion" is my Swan Song!

KELSEY: "Maid Marion" is my Holy Grail!

(PROCTOR enters)

PROCTOR: Okay, thanks for waiting. You all must be very excited, but before we get started I have one minor announcement to make. The role of Robin Hood is now open to both males <u>and</u> females. So ladies, if you'd like to try for this role instead, feel free to sign up for the new lead role here. Thanks!

(PROCTOR places a clipboard on the table and exits. The girls stare, flabbergasted at the clipboard)

EMILY & KELSEY: *(Whispered amazement)* Robin Hood?

(Both girls jump at the clipboard and fight each other off to be the first to sign up)

BLACKOUT

"We're expecting 16 hurricanes today, so local schools have been delayed by one hour."

SO YOU THINK YOU CAN NEWS

(Lights up on our announcer, ELIZABETH, who is flanked by our two contestants, LULU and KAI)

ELIZABETH: Welcome back to another exciting episode of "So You Think You Can News"! I'm your host, Elizabeth Stokely. We're down to our final two contestants, Lulu and Kai.

LULU: Welcome back to another exciting episode of "So You Think You--

ELIZABETH: Lulu! That's *my* cue card. You don't have one.

LULU: Then how will I know what to say?

ELIZABETH: *(Back to audience)* Perfect news anchor material, isn't she folks? And here we have Kai.

KAI: Thanks, Lizzy.

So You Think You Can News

ELIZABETH: It's Elizabeth.

KAI: Thanks, Beth.

ELIZABETH: Moving on. Our two contestants will have to navigate a series of news anchor obstacles, to see who will be crowned the title of Lead Anchor. First up is Kai, with the dreaded Post-Game Interview.

KAI: Thanks, Ellie.

ELIZABETH: I'm going to kill you.

(JOHNNY LIGHTS, a professional football player enters. KAI crosses to him)

KAI: I'm here with the winning quarterback, Johnny Lights. Johnny, how do you feel right now?

JOHNNY: Oh man. It's just... I mean... All the guys out there... and the fans... we figured we had to... but then... *(exhales and nods his head)* one game at a time.

KAI: Okay, what went through your head during that last play?

JOHNNY: The coach was key. Our team worked so hard in the off-season. We just gotta keep our eyes on the prize. I mean, everyone out there did their job. *(Exhales and nods his head)* One game at a time.

KAI: Didn't even come close to answering my question. What do you think about that controversial call, late in the 4th quarter?

JOHNNY: I'm just happy to be here. Hope I can make a difference--

KAI: But what about that call in the 4th?

So You Think You Can News   *Joshua Evans*

JOHNNY: Defense wins championships, and I just wanna give it 110%--

KAI: The call in the 4th!

JOHNNY: We brought our "A" game today--

KAI: The call!!!

JOHNNY: *(Exhales and nods his head)* One game at a time.

(JOHNNY LIGHTS exits, and KAI joins ELIZABETH and LULU again)

ELIZABETH: Tough round, Kai.

KAI: Thanks, Betty.

ELIZABETH: E-Liz-A-Beth.

KAI: *(Winks and points at her)* Back to you.

ELIZABETH: Next up is Lulu with our unique Proud Parents Challenge. Lulu, please have a seat in our anchor chair, and do your best to read the news to camera.

(LULU takes a seat)

LULU: Our top story tonight: Police in Dylanware are still on the lookout for the elusive Pet Snatcher.

(GEORGE, played by the same actor who played JOHNNY LIGHTS, and MARTHA enter)

MARTHA: Oh, there she is! Lulu...! Honey...! Surprise! We drove all the way from Clarkston.

So You Think You Can News

GEORGE: There's my Big Girl! We thought we'd surprise you at work. Traffic was murder.

LULU: *(Doing her best not get distracted)* Responsible for over 15 cases of stealing pets, the Pet Snatcher is believed to be--

MARTHA: What ever happened to that nice boy you were dating? Lance? Vance?

GEORGE: Pumpkin, does this look like a rash to you? Your mother and I can't tell.

MARTHA: You never call anymore. Is your phone broken, or do you just hate me that much?

GEORGE: I tried The Google yesterday, and now my darn computer won't start up.

LULU: *(Focused, but getting more agitated)* Authorities are asking people in the neighborhood to lock up their pets and keep an eye out for any--

MARTHA: You know that young man you work with? I showed him some of your baby pictures.

GEORGE: I know you don't like calling your mother, but if you ever need to talk, I'm here for you too. *(Whispers)* Even if it's girl talk.

LULU: *(Really straining)* The Pet Snatcher... was... last seen--

MARTHA: Look, here's a picture of you taking a bath in the kitchen sink. Remember when you were skinny?

GEORGE: Oh! Kevin stopped by. He said that your number changed, so I went ahead and gave him your new phone number...

So You Think You Can News   Joshua Evans

LULU: *(Loses it)* Kevin?! You gave Kevin my new number?! Kevin?! Did you ever stop to think about why I changed my number in the first place? Hmmm?!! Maybe I was trying to avoid someone...?!

GEORGE: ...Kevin?

LULU: Kevin!!!

MARTHA: Don't yell, sweetheart, you know it makes your chin break out in pimples.

(LULU yells to the sky, and crosses back to ELIZABETH and KAI. MARTHA and GEORGE exit)

ELIZABETH: Yikes. That didn't go well. Sorry Lulu.

LULU: *(Completely flummoxed)* Words. Words!... *(collects herself)* Words are hard right now.

ELIZABETH: I can imagine. Next up is Kai, with our Bleepin' Chef. Take it away, Kai.

KAI: Thanks, Beth-Ann.

ELIZABETH: Uuuuugh!!

(CHEF MANN, played by the same actor who played MARTHJA, enters)

CHEF MANN: *(British accent)* Welcome to cooking with Chef Mann. I'm Chef Mann, and I'm the man. Today I'm cooking on this willy-knock of a news show with this punky little anchor.

KAI: Hello. I'm here to make sure our audience at home doesn't hear your dirty mouth.

So You Think You Can News

CHEF MANN: Good luck, you little <u>parferoy</u>. *(All underlined words are "Bleeped" by KAI)*

KAI: Good start. What's on the menu for today?

CHEF MANN: We'll be taking a stunning frosting, and adding it to these delicious <u>blarking</u> doughnuts.

KAI: Almost slipped that one past me there.

CHEF MANN: You mother was a <u>mixtifferon</u> of a <u>flaxfont</u>.

KAI: I don't think we need to bring my mother into this.

CHEF MANN: You whiny little <u>blarxfit</u>. I'll take these <u>shongding</u> doughnuts, shove them down your <u>tropple</u> throat. Your <u>rantoont</u> of a mother won't even recognize your <u>maggleton</u> of a face, you <u>derdenton</u> excuse for a <u>marxinton</u> news anchor. Now get the <u>conxt</u> out of my way.

KAI: Anything else?

CHEF MANN: Beetle-fart.

KAI: *(Looks at ELIZABETH)* Can we allow beetle-fart? *(ELIZABETH gives a thumbs up)* Beetle-fart indeed! Thanks for joining us, Chef Mann.

CHEF MANN: I'm Chef Mann, and I'm the man.

(KAI crosses to ELIZABETH and LULU, while CHEF MANN exits)

ELIZABETH: Well done, Kai! That is definitely not an easy challenge.

KAI: Thanks, Jenny.

So You Think You Can News   <small>Joshua Evans</small>

ELIZABETH: That's not even close to my name. *(Turns to camera)* Our final challenge today will be for Lulu. And we've saved the best for last: our world-famous Weather Report.

LULU: Our world-famous Weather Report.

ELIZABETH: *(Smacking LULU with her index cards)* That's my line, you dum-dum!

(LULU crosses away. WEATHER 1 [JOHNNY LIGHTS / GEORGE] and WEATHER 2 [MARTHA / CHEF MANN] enter with a box, and stand next to her)

ELIZABETH: First up: Los Angeles.

LULU: Our Severe Weather Watch continues, as we come together as a city to try to make it through this storm. Angelenos have been scared into hiding due to the 3 mile per hour wind, and we have reports of five (yes *five*) raindrops that have fallen in the Valleys.

(WEATHER 1 and WEATHER 2 each spray her shirt once with a squirt bottle)

LULU: Oh! I've been hit! Yes, breaking news! I can confirm that I have just been hit by not one, but *two* raindrops. I'm seeing traffic come to a screeching halt, and people everywhere are canceling their plans.

ELIZABETH: Not bad, not bad. Next round: Orlando.

LULU: *(Slightly nervous)* Orlando?

WEATHER 1 / WEATHER 2: Orlando.

(WEATHER 1 and WEATHER 2 begin to relentlessly spray LULU with the squirt bottles)

So You Think You Can News

LULU: Another typical Winter Tuesday here in Orlando. I think it might be raining, but I really can't tell. The humidity is so high that rain and air have become one. We're expecting 16 hurricanes today, so local schools have been delayed by one hour.

ELIZABETH: Excellent. Now it's time for the Final Round.

LULU: *(Scared)* Where?

WEATHER 1 / WEATHER 2: Oklahoma City!

(WEATHER 1 and WEATHER 2 begin throwing numerous pillows at LULU)

LULU: I'm here in Oklahoma City outside of a Big Bill's Pillow Outlet! Tornado Charlie has ripped this outlet store apart, and has sent pillows everywhere!

(WEATHER 1 and WEATHER 2 stop throwing pillows, and straight-up just start smacking LULU with pillows across the body)

LULU: Residents have reported pillows splitting trees in half, and demolishing trailer parks. We'll keep you updated on this deadly storm! Back to you!

(WEATHER 1 and WEATHER 2 immediately stop, drop their pillows, and golf clap for LULU. ELIZABETH and KAI applaud LULU as she crosses back to them)

ELIZABETH: Absolutely amazing! I think it's clear who our winner is: Lulu! We'll see you next time on, "So You Think You Can News"!

BLACKOUT

"Mom always told us, 'Better to be afraid of the dark, than to get eaten by penguins.'"

*T*RAPPED

(Lights up on SUE, RAY, BETH, and MEGAN sitting on stage. Silence. After a beat, BETH calmly rises, brushes herself off and calms herself. She takes a deep breath, and with a yell, runs off SR)

BETH: Aaaaaaaaaah!

MEGAN: *(Calling after her)* It won't do any good.

(BETH reappears from SL)

SUE: We told you… there's no escaping this place.

RAY: …or would you like to try **yet again**?

BETH: I can't take it any longer!

MEGAN: Face it, guys: we're stuck here. Stupid evil magician.

BETH: There's got to be a way out!

SUE: There isn't, so stop trying.

Trapped

RAY: That evil magician trapped us down here, and he's never gonna let us go.

SUE: I hate evil magicians.

RAY: They're the worst.

MEGAN: We're gonna die here.

BETH: I'm not gonna die here!

SUE: Oh, what makes you so special?

RAY: Yeah, are you gonna run yourself outta here? We already saw how successful that was.

BETH: I can't just sit here! *(Pointing towards the audience)* What's down that way?

MEGAN: Who knows? It's really dark, so we may never know.

SUE: Mom always told us, "Better to be afraid of the dark, than to get eaten by penguins."

MEGAN: Mom was weird.

RAY: She never got eaten by penguins though.

(RAY, MEGAN, and SUE all nod in agreement)

BETH: Forget Mom's crazy advice! Let's go that way and see if there's a way out!

RAY: Are you nuts?!!

SUE: Go somewhere that's dark?

Trapped   *Joshua Evans*

BETH: Why not?

MEGAN: Penguins, dude.

RAY / SUE: Penguins.

BETH: This is ridiculous.

MEGAN: So is all this talk of dark places. I'm not going anywhere near them.

SUE: No… we're gonna die here unless we do something drastic.

BETH: Drastic?

MEGAN: I think I know where you're going with this.

RAY: Yes. It's tough, but it's time.

BETH: What are you guys talking about?

SUE: If we're gonna survive here, we're gonna have to eat someone.

BETH: What?

MEGAN: She's right.

BETH: No!

RAY: There's no other way.

BETH: Yes there is! *(Pointing towards the audience)* We go towards the darkness!

SUE: Beth. We talked about this.

Trapped

BETH: You'd rather eat one of us, than explore a dark place?!!

MEGAN: It's the only way.

BETH: You guys are nuts!

RAY: I vote we eat Beth.

SUE: I second that.

MEGAN: Sounds like a vote has been called.

BETH: No! There's no vote!

RAY: Discussion on the issue? *(SUE raises her hand)* Sue?

SUE: Thank you. I think it only makes sense to eat Beth first.

BETH: Why?!

SUE: She's in favor of the dark.

RAY: Good point.

BETH: No! Bad point!

MEGAN: A vote has been called.

BETH: You guys are crazy! I'm trying the dark area.

SUE: Please, Beth. We're trying to have a vote here.

BETH: Vote then! I'm outta here.

(BETH makes her way towards the audience)

Trapped *Joshua Evans*

RAY: All those in favor of eating Beth first…

BETH: Here goes nothing…

(BETH runs into the audience, and out into the lobby)

RAY / SUE / MEGAN: Aye.

RAY: Motion passes.

MEGAN: Sorry Beth. Beth? Beth?

SUE: I nominate we eat Megan first.

RAY: Second.

MEGAN: Wait… what?

BLACKOUT

"Kitchen Floor?! Oh no no no no no no... I'm not supposed to be here."

KITCHEN FLOOR

(Lights up on DIRT, Q-TIP, and OLD MAN RAISIN. DIRT is sitting on the ground, while Q-TIP lies motionless. OLD MAN RAISIN sits in the corner alone. He has a long beard, and he wears a cloak with the hood pulled up. Suddenly, CHEERIO comes crashing on stage)

CHEERIO: Whoa!

(None of the other characters pay CHEERIO much attention. CHEERIO looks around, confused)

CHEERIO: Wait... where am I? This isn't the cereal bowl.

Q-TIP: D-duh!

DIRT: Can it, Q-Tip. Give the kid some space.

CHEERIO: Q-Tip? I don't belong with a Q-Tip.

Q-TIP: *(Jumps up and hops over to CHEERIO)* You got a problem with me?! What, you're too good to be seen with a bathroom accessory?!

Kitchen Floor

DIRT: *(Pushing Q-TIP down with ease)* I said leave him alone.

CHEERIO: What's going on? Where am I? And where are all my brothers and sisters?

OLD MAN RAISIN: You are forever lost, Round One.

DIRT: Old Man Raisin is right: you're officially lost, just like the rest of us. Welcome to the Kitchen Floor.

CHEERIO: Kitchen Floor?! Oh no no no no no no... I'm not supposed to be here.

Q-TIP: How do you think I feel? I'm in the wrong room completely!

DIRT: Listen kid, what's your name?

CHEERIO: I'm Cheerio.

DIRT: Well Cheerio, I'm Dirt. The hot-head is Q-Tip, and the quiet one over there is Old Man Raisin.

(DUSTY enters, seemingly to float above everyone else)

DUSTY: The End is near. Beware the End.

Q-TIP: Shut up, Dusty!

DUSTY: Oh, hey guys.

DIRT: And that's Dusty. She kinda comes in and out. *(Whispers)* She's a little light-headed.

DUSTY: *(To CHEERIO)* The End is coming...

Kitchen Floor *Joshua Evans*

CHEERIO: What's going on here? I'm only supposed to be in a box or a bowl. Not here!

OLD MAN RAISIN: We all have to be somewhere. Maybe <u>Here</u> is not supposed to be with <u>You</u>.

(DUSTY floats off)

Q-TIP: Oh great, the Old Man is philosophizing again.

OLD MAN RAISIN: Heal the young one's fears.

DIRT: He's right. *(To CHEERIO)* You gotta calm down, little buddy.

CHEERIO: *(Starting to lose it)* But I'm not supposed to be here.

Q-TIP: Sing it, sista'!

CHEERIO: I'm not supposed to be here.

OLD MAN RAISIN: And yet, here you are.

CHEERIO: *(Exploding)* I'm not supposed to be here!

(This outburst silences the room. DUSTY floats back in)

DUSTY: Beware the End.

Q-TIP: Shut up, Dusty!

DUSTY: Oh, hey guys.

CHEERIO: This is a mistake. I need to get back up to the kitchen counter.

Kitchen Floor

Q-TIP: The kitchen counter?! HA!

DIRT: He's right. Once you end up down here, you're stuck here.

CHEERIO: For how long?

Q-TIP: Forever!

DUSTY: Until the world ends.

Q-TIP: Go away, Dusty!

(Q-TIP gives a hard blow towards DUSTY, which sends her flying off-stage)

CHEERIO: How long have you all been down here?

DIRT: Too long. But nobody as long as Old Man Raisin.

Q-TIP: How about it, old man? How long you been here?

OLD MAN RAISIN: Many fort-mops have passed since my existence here.

CHEERIO: "Fort-Mops"?

DIRT: That's fourteen times the owners have mopped the floor.

CHEERIO: *(In shock of OLD MAN RAISIN)* Really?

OLD MAN RAISIN: When I first entered this realm, I was not a raisin at all.

Q-TIP: Is this some past-life nonsense?

OLD MAN RAISIN: Nay. I used to be young. When first I landed here, I was a glorious purple grape.

CHEERIO / Q-TIP / DIRT: Whoa...

(DUSTY enters)

DUSTY: Do you hear the End?

Q-TIP: I'm gonna kill her!

(Q-TIP tries, in vain, to swat at DUSTY)

DUSTY: You cannot stop the End of the World.

Q-TIP: But I can stop you from blabbering!

DIRT: Q-Tip, stop. Listen. I actually hear something.

(Q-TIP stops. A slight rumble is heard off-stage. It gets increasing louder)

CHEERIO: I hear it too.

Q-TIP: What is that?

DUSTY: The End is here!

DIRT: It's getting closer.

CHEERIO: What should we do?

OLD MAN RAISIN: *(Rises and joins the others)* Accept our Fate, my friends.

Q-TIP: Dirt... I'm scared.

Kitchen Floor

DUSTY: The End is HERE!

DIRT: Where?!

DUSTY: *(Points off-stage)* There!

(A giant conglomerate of six or seven actors come bounding on-stage. They are linked together arm in arm, and with various pieces of trash. They slowly make their way towards the group)

DIRT / Q-TIP: **DUST BUNNY!!**

CHEERIO: Should we run?!

DIRT: Too late!

(DIRT, Q-TIP, OLD MAN RAISIN, and CHEERIO are frozen in terror as the Dust Bunny makes it's way towards them. It soon overtakes them, and consumes them into their collective, amid much yelling. The new, larger Dust Bunny rolls off-stage, leaving DUSTY alone)

DUSTY: Told you. *(Beat)* I wonder what's happening in the living room.

(DUSTY floats off)

BLACKOUT

*"I was just thinking the exact same thought. The city **is** beautiful, and I am perfect."*

ATLANTIS!

(Lights up on ARCHIBALD sitting at an outdoor cafe, enjoying the beautiful day)

ARCHIBALD: What a wonderful day. How could the day *not* be wonderful, here in... ***Atlantis***?!

(CORNELIUS enters)

CORNELIUS: Why Archibald, how the devil are you?

ARCHIBALD: Cornelius! I'm good. I'm very, *very* good! Take a look around: the city is beautiful, and I am perfect!

CORNELIUS: I was just thinking the exact same thought. The city *is* beautiful, and *I* am perfect.

ARCHIBALD: Yes, and do you know why...?

CORNELIUS: Because everything is perfect in...

ARCHIBALD / CORNELIUS: ...***Atlantis***!

Atlantis!

(They both laugh heartily)

ARCHIBALD: Enjoy this day with me. Have a drink.

CORNELIUS: Of course! *(He takes a drink)* I say, what is this?

ARCHIBALD: It's called coffee.

CORNELIUS: Egad! We've invented coffee already?

ARCHIBALD: Splendid, isn't it?

(CORNELIUS takes out some chocolate)

CORNELIUS: *(Offers some chocolate to ARCHIBALD)* Would you like some?

ARCHIBALD: Of course! *(He eats a bite)* My word, what is this?

CORNELIUS: It's called chocolate. We just invented it.

ARCHIBALD: In the timespan of two minutes, you and I have invented coffee and chocolate?

CORNELIUS: It appears so.

ARCHIBALD / CORNELIUS: *Atlantis*!

(THADEOUS enters)

THADEOUS: Archibald! Cornelius!

ARCHIBALD / CORNELIUS: Thadeous!

THADEOUS: May I tell you my good news? I've started a new career.

Atlantis! Joshua Evans

ARCHIBALD: Do tell!

THADEOUS: People now pay me money to draw portaits of them.

CORNELIUS: And you can earn a living off of these silly scribblings?

THADEOUS: Apparently so. I've decided to call it "Art".

ARCHIBALD: You've invented Art?

THADEOUS: Gadzooks, I believe I just did.

ARCHIBALD / CORNELIUS / THADEOUS: *Atlantis*!

THADEOUS: May I draw you two?

ARCHIBALD: *(Indicating himself and CORNELIUS)* These two stunning subjects?

CORNELIUS: I'm amazed you haven't started already.

(THADEOUS begins to sketch them)

ARCHIBALD: Can you believe the Egyptians are still making their silly pyramids in the desert?

CORNELIUS: Ha! Yes! Those will never last!

THADEOUS: Viola! *(Shows them the picture)* Thoughts?

ARCHIBALD: ...My word!! ...I'm gorgeous!

CORNELIUS: I can't stop looking at me!

THADEOUS: And now, I shall draw the background.

Atlantis!

(THADEOUS begins to sketch again)

CORNELIUS: Would you like to meet my robot dog?

ARCHIBALD: You've mastered robotics?

CORNELIUS: Just his morning. *(Calls offstage)* Rover!

(ROVER, the robot dog, enters)

ROVER: *(In a robotic voice)* Woof. Woof.

ARCHIBALD: Well done!

ROVER: Woof. Woof. Why couldn't the skeleton cross the road? Because it didn't have the **guts**.

CORNELIUS: Googely-Moogely! Did my robot just invent humor?

ROVER: What do clouds wear under their shorts? Thunder-wear.

THADEOUS: Finished!

(THADEOUS shows them his painting)

ARCHIBALD: I say, Thadeous... what's that you've drawn behind us?

THADEOUS: That's the giant meteor that's hurtling towards us.

(All four turn to look at the meteor. Long beat)

ARCHIBALD: So it is.

ROVER: Did you hear about the fire at the circus? It was intense. Woof. Woof. In-**tents**.

Atlantis!   Joshua Evans

CORNELIUS: Isn't Atlantis amazing?

THADEOUS: Coffee, chocolate...

ARCHIBALD: Art, comedic robot dogs...

CORNELIUS: And now... our very own meteor racing towards our great city.

ARCHIBALD: Even the *heavens* know we're amazing.

THADEOUS: Of course they do. After all, this is...

ALL: *Atlantis*!

CORNELIUS: What could possibly go wrong?

BLACKOUT

"Listen... if you eat that sandwich, terrible stuff is gonna happen to us."

*S*ANDWICH

(Lights up on a small table and a chair. On the table is a plate with a sandwich on it. ROBIN casually walks onstage. She walks past the sandwich, but, keeping her same stride and pace, comes back to it. She is surprised at the perfect presentation of the whole scene, with no one around to claim this delectable meal. She looks around. She sees no one. She waits for another beat, then sits down to enjoy the sandwich)

ROBIN: Don't mind if I do...

(She lifts the sandwich to her mouth, savoring the first bite. But before she can sink her teeth in, FUTURE ROBIN runs in)

FUTURE ROBIN: Wait!!

(This stops ROBIN cold in her tracks. As FUTURE ROBIN is behind ROBIN, she cannot tell who yelled at her. She is frozen, sandwich to mouth)

FUTURE ROBIN: *(Coming around to face ROBIN dead on)* Don't do it!

Sandwich

(ROBIN is confused at what she is looking at)

ROBIN: You're me.

FUTURE ROBIN: And you're me.

ROBIN: How's that possible?

FUTURE ROBIN: Time travel.

ROBIN: Awesome.

FUTURE ROBIN: Totally.

ROBIN: Future?

FUTURE ROBIN: Yup.

ROBIN: Good news or bad news?

FUTURE ROBIN: Bad news.

ROBIN: Bummer.

FUTURE ROBIN: Listen... if you eat that sandwich, terrible stuff is gonna happen to us.

ROBIN: But I love sandwiches.

FUTURE ROBIN: Don't I know it.

ROBIN: Bad news? You sure?

FUTURE ROBIN: *(Points at herself)* Future.

ROBIN: *(Sighs, and puts down the sandwich)* Okaaaaaaay...

Sandwich Joshua Evans

FUTURE ROBIN: Good work.

ROBIN: See you soon.

FUTURE ROBIN: *(Smiles and points at ROBIN)* Aaaaah! Time travel joke...

ROBIN: We're funny...

(FUTURE ROBIN gives a salute, which ROBIN matches. And with that, FUTURE ROBIN exits. ROBIN begins to exit the opposite way, but stops. She does a small "pee-pee dance" as she debates what to do. Hunger gets the best of her, and she returns to the table. Once there, she takes a huge bite out of the sandwich. FUTURE ROBIN comes bursting onstage, this time wearing an eye patch and her arm in a sling)

FUTURE ROBIN: Whoa!

ROBIN: Oooohhh... right! I forgot.

FUTURE ROBIN: Look! *(Grabs ROBIN by the shoulder)* This sandwich is a trap. Set by an evil, dark witch who does terrible terrible things.

ROBIN: Evil?

FUTURE ROBIN: *(Holds up her arm sling)* ...and dark.

ROBIN: No more sandwich... you got it!

(ROBIN gives a salute, unfortunately it's with FUTURE ROBIN'S bad arm, which FUTURE ROBIN tries to match. FUTURE ROBIN exits. ROBIN smiles, and decides to leave. She stops a few steps in and turns back to the sandwich)

Sandwich

ROBIN: *(Holding up her hands like weights on a scale)* Broken arm... Sandwich. Eye patch... Sandwich. *(Tipping the scales for the winner)* Sandwich!

(She rushes back to the table, and takes a huge bite out of the sandwich. FUTURE ROBIN again comes bursting onto the stage, this time on crutches and wearing a helmet)

FUTURE ROBIN: DUDE!!!

ROBIN: *(Genuinely forgetful and sorry)* Oh, right! Right! I'm so sorry! Totally my bad.

FUTURE ROBIN: Perhaps I wasn't clear... *(Indicates her entire broken body)* EVIL WITCH!

ROBIN: *(Thumbs up, nodding her head)* Evil Witch. Broken bones. One good eye. Check check double check. My bad. Totally my bad.

FUTURE ROBIN: Come on, man! What's it gonna take?!! You have no idea what that witch is capable of!!

(ROBIN tries to give the salute, but FUTURE ROBIN can't manage a return salute due to her crutches. She exits. ROBIN has already forgotten all about her, as she is now sock puppet fighting with her two empty hands. After the puppets turn on her, she drops them, and notice the sandwich)

ROBIN: Oh! A sandwich!

(ROBIN takes another huge bite. FUTURE ROBIN, no longer in crutches or bandages, but this time played by grown man, comes bounding onstage)

FUTURE ROBIN: Now look what you did to us!!!

Sandwich *Joshua Evans*

ROBIN: *(Drops the sandwich in disgust)* Aaaaaaaah! *(She stares at FUTURE ROBIN for a bit, maybe even touching his face to make sure he's real. Then she notices the sandwich on the floor)* Oh! A sandwich!

(She reaches down to pick up the sandwich. FUTURE ROBIN storms out)

BLACKOUT

"Captain, I don't think we should trust these savages."

Isla Peligroso – 1839

(Lights up on CAPTAIN LUXFORD, his wife, LADY SCARLET, and First Mate MR. WILLIS)

MR. WILLIS: Captain Luxford, after six months at sea, we've finally arrived... Isla Peligroso.

CAPTAIN LUXFORD: *(To LADY SCARLET)* Oh Darling, isn't it beautiful?

LADY SCARLET: *(Staring at MR. WILLIS)* He certainly is.

MR. WILLIS: *(Noticing LADY SCARLET, but trying to ignore her)* Yes, well... I'm sure that you and your beautiful new wife, Lady Scarlet, will be very happy here.

CAPTAIN LUXFORD: Why do they call it Isla Peligroso, Mr. Willis?

MR. WILLIS: It translates to Danger Island, sir, but no one knows the reason. It's one of the island's many secrets.

Isla Peligroso – 1839

LADY SCARLET: *(To MR. WILLIS)* I like secrets... *(She silently growls at him).*

CAPTAIN LUXFORD: Mr. Willis, you have done a wonderful job, and I am pleased to have had you as my First Mate.

MR. WILLIS: Thank you, Sir.

CAPTAIN LUXFORD: I would be honored if you would stay here, and help us build our home.

LADY SCARLET: Oh please stay, Mr. Willis. Please?! A strange island... *(indicating the a possible romance between the two of them)* ....there might **be** something here.

MR. WILLIS: I'm sorry, Lady Scarlet, **there's nothing here.**

LADY SCARLET: But something might **happen**.

MR. WILLIS: **Not gonna happen**.

LADY SCARLET: No?

MR. WILLIS: No.

LADY SCARLET: Maybe?

MR. WILLIS: Never.

LADY SCARLET: *(Coyly)* We'll see...

CAPTAIN LUXFORD: *(Looking off)* Did you hear something?

(Two islanders, LOOMBA and BEMBE, enter)

MR. WILLIS: *(Jumping in front to protect them)* Get back, Sir!

Isla Peligroso – 1839
Joshua Evans

CAPTAIN LUXFORD: Nonesense, Mr. Willis. It's just two natives. *(To them)* I say, hello there!

LOOMBA: Welcome, Strangers.

CAPTAIN LUXFORD: You speak English, wonderful!

BEMBE: Very glad to have you here.

MR. WILLIS: Who are you?

LOOMBA: *(Patting himself)* Loomba. Island Chief.

BEMBE: *(Patting himself)* Bembe. Island Cook.

LADY SCARLET: Cook?

BEMBE: *(Catching himself)* No! ...um... doctor.

CAPTAIN LUXFORD: A doctor? Wonderful! I'm Captain Luxford.

MR. WILLIS: Captain, I don't think we should trust these savages.

CAPTAIN LUXFORD: Why not?

MR. WILLIS: I believe that they're cannibals, Sir.

LOOMBA: *(Spoken)* Shock!

BEMBE: *(Spoken)* Gasp!

LADY SCARLET: You're so smart, Mr. Willis. How could you tell?

MR. WILLIS: They're literally wearing human skulls as necklaces.

Isla Peligroso – 1839

LOOMBA: *(Spoken)* Laughter, laughter, laughter.

BEMBE: Much amusement.

LOOMBA: No, no, no... these are monkey skulls.

CAPTAIN LUXFORD: Yes, of course: monkey skulls! Mr. Willis, you should be ashamed.

LADY SCARLET: You're absolutely right, Darling. Maybe I should take Mr. Willis back to the ship, and have a long, private conversation with him...

MR. WILLIS: No, that definitely won't be necessary. I just... *(Looking at the islanders)* Are you putting salt on the Captain?

LOOMBA & BEMBE: Whaaaaaaaaaat?

MR. WILLIS: *(Tasting the salt)* This is salt and pepper...

BEMBE: ...and paprika.

LOOMBA: Yes. Ancient Island Tradition: Increases luck.

BEMBE: ...and tastiness.

MR. WILLIS: What?

LOOMBA: What?

MR. WILLIS: Did you--

BEMBE: No.

MR. WILLIS: Captain, I must insist that we leave at once. These savages mean to do you harm.

Isla Peligroso – 1839   Joshua Evans

CAPTAIN LUXFORD: Mr. Willis! You will stand down at once. These natives have come to welcome us, and you are being extremely rude. This simply will not stand! I will not have your insubordination--

MR. WILLIS: Sir.

CAPTAIN LUXFORD: Don't interrupt me, Mr. Willis!

MR. WILLIS: They're building a fire at your feet.

LOOMBA: Honorary Welcome Fire.

BEMBE: Big feast planned.

CAPTAIN LUXFORD: Am I the Guest of Honor?

BEMBE: Of course.

LOOMBA: Main course.

LADY SCARLET: *(Finally understanding what's about to happen)* Mr. Willis, I *really* think we *should* let the natives welcome my husband.

MR. WILLIS: *(Shocked)* Lady Scarlet!

CAPTAIN LUXFORD: Thank you, Darling.

MR. WILLIS: Sir, I strongly feel that--

BEMBE: Bite down on apple, please.

LOOMBA: Ancient tradition.

   (CAPTAIN LUXFORD bites down on the apple, then gives MR.

Isla Peligroso – 1839

WILLIS a thumbs up)

MR. WILLIS: *(Giving up)* Good luck, Captain.

(MR. WILLIS exits)

LADY SCARLET: *(Looking at her husband)* Mr. Willis, after this dinner, can we talk about your plans for staying?

(She exits after him)

LOOMBA: They left in hurry.

BEMBE: No worries. Fast food not good for you anyways.

BLACKOUT

"Don't be stupid: we know what happens when someone touches the mirror."

A Saturday Afternoon

(Lights up on an attic. There are random pieces of furniture scattered across the stage, covered with white sheets. The stage is split into a mirror images of itself, with the furniture placed specifically identical to its counterpart. A sheet covers a long "mirror" center stage, dividing the room. Erik Satie's "Gnossienne No. 4" begins to play. SONJA, WILL, AARON, and PENNY enter. From across the stage, STEVE, WARREN, ANTHONY, and PERCY enter. Like the stage, they are mirror images of each other. While the first group is modernly dressed, the second group has a distinct 1950s look to them. When the first group speaks, the second group does not mouth their words)

SONJA: Wow...

WILL: I told you.

AARON: Junior, this place is awesome.

PENNY: Grandpa William was right.

SONJA: Your grandpa you're named after? He knew this old guy?

A Saturday Afternoon

WILL: No, he didn't really know him. He just knew *of* him.

AARON: How long has the guy been dead?

PENNY: A couple dozen years or so.

SONJA: I wonder why they haven't bulldozed this place down then.

WILL: This place is so far back in the woods, nobody even knows it's here.

AARON: And this attic looks like it's the only room with stuff still in it.

PENNY: Grandpa William said that when they were teenagers, they sometimes liked to sneak in here.

SONJA: To a creepy old dude's attic?

WILL: Yeah, but he told us to stay away... no matter what.

AARON: That's weird. Why?

PENNY: He never told me and Willliam. He didn't like to talk about this place.

(SONJA pulls at the sheet center stage)

SONJA: Whoa, look at this.

(AARON comes over to check it out)

AARON: Cool. It's like some kind of trick mirror or something.

SONJA: How is still turned on after all these years?

A Saturday Afternoon Joshua Evans

PENNY: What do you mean, "turned on"?

AARON: Look at it. The reflection is of us, but it's changed our clothes to look all old.

WILL: *(Coming over with PENNY to check it out)* What?

SONJA: Check it out, Junior, it moves with us, but it's changed how we look.

AARON: That's crazy.

WILL: I wonder how it does that.

AARON: It's probably some computer chip or something.

PENNY: No way, this place hasn't been touched in decades. They didn't have this kind of technology back then.

(WILL reaches out to touch the mirror, touching WARREN)

WILL: Whoa, it feels weird.

PENNY: William...

WILL: No, really. Feel it.

SONJA: Really?

(PENNY, SONJA, and AARON reach out to their counterparts. The next four lines are said as the eight characters switch places with each other, in a slow, mirrored movement)

PENNY: That's super weird.

AARON: Oh man, that's strange.

A Saturday Afternoon

WILL: Right? I told you.

SONJA: What is this made of, William?

(The two groups have now completely switched sides of the stage, having traveled through the mirror. WILL begins to move away from the mirror, but his counterpart, WARREN, doesn't move with him. WILL is talking, but no sound is heard by the audience. WILL's group is now mute, although they still talk and hear each other. AARON moves off the mirror as well, and his counterpart, ANTHONY, doesn't move either. None of the counterparts are moving now. SONJA raises her finger, and taps on the glass, wondering why the reflections aren't moving anymore)

WARREN: Did it work?

(SONJA and PENNY jump back, startled)

ANTHONY: Get your hands away!

(He reaches out and pulls STEVE and PERCY's hands away from the mirror)

PERCY: Are we free?

STEVE: It worked!

WARREN: We're out!

ANTHONY: We're finally free!

PERCY: Who took our place?

(They look to the mirror)

STEVE: It must be them.

A Saturday Afternoon   *Joshua Evans*

(STEVE, WARREN, ANTHONY, and PERCY all examine their counterparts in the mirror. While SONJA, WILL, AARON, and PENNY are not mirroring their movements, they too are examining their reflection. No sound can be heard from SONJA's group)

WARREN: Careful! Don't get too close.

ANTHONY: Don't let them touch you.

PERCY: Don't be stupid: we *know* what happens when someone touches the mirror.

STEVE: How long have we been trapped in there?

WARREN: Too many years to count.

ANTHONY: But we haven't aged a day.

PERCY: Not since we got sucked into that thing.

STEVE: And that chicken, William, ran away and left us.

WARREN: He's gotta be a grandpa by now...

ANTHONY: Do we just leave?

PERCY: The four kids who pulled *us* in just left.

STEVE: We've gotta destroy this thing.

WARREN: Smash it to pieces.

ANTHONY: What?! We can't do that to these kids.

PERCY: If we break it, we have no idea what will happen to them.

A Saturday Afternoon

STEVE: So we just sit back, knowing that some other kid is going to get sucked in there?

WARREN: *(Pointing to the mirror group)* They're going to figure out some way to trick some kids to touch the mirror.

ANTHONY: *(Not proud of his actions)* ...just like we did.

PERCY: ...It'll keep on going... over and over...

(STEVE grabs a heavy object, intending to smash the mirror)

STEVE: This ends now.

(ANTHONY jumps in front of STEVE, blocking his throw)

ANTHONY: Steve, no!

WARREN: Do it, Steve!

PERCY: *(Joining ANTHONY, pleading with STEVE)* If you do this, you'll regret it forever. Stop, and think.

(STEVE thinks about it for a long moment, then defiantly drops the object)

STEVE: Fine. *(Points at the mirror)* But this... *thing*... it's on your head. Not mine.

(STEVE exits)

WARREN: I'm outta here.

ANTHONY: But what about these kids?

WARREN: Better them, than me.

A Saturday Afternoon *Joshua Evans*

(WARREN exits)

ANTHONY: *(Looking at the new foursome trapped in the mirror)* I'm sorry.

PERCY: We'll try to send some kids your way eventually.

ANTHONY: C'mon, let's go.

PERCY: It's weird... *(points to WILL)* That one looks just like William.

(ANTHONY and PERCY exit, leaving PENNY, WILL, SONJA, and AARON silently banging on the mirror, trying desperately to escape)

BLACKOUT

"Where we sit today… here, now… will totally determine the rest of our lives."

TOTALLY

(JANE and JANINE enter, carrying their lunches)

JANE: Wow. Our first High School Lunch! Aren't you excited?!

JANINE: Totally stoked!

JANE: I know, right?!

JANINE: Totally!

JANE: I know, right?!

JANINE: Totally!

JANE: Okay… let's not blow this. Where we sit today… here, now… will totally determine the rest of our lives.

JANINE: Totally!

JANE: I know, right?!

Totally

JANINE: *(Looking around)* So... where should we sit?

JANE: I don't know... *(Pointing)* How about over there?

JANINE: *(Slaps her hand down)* Totally not!

JANE: Why? What have you heard?

JANINE: That's Tommy Smith sitting with those guys!

JANE: So?

JANINE: "So?" You didn't hear? Sara told Amy, who heard from Susan, who sweet-talked Greg, who eavesdropped on Ryan that Tommy once picked his nose on the bus last year... and ate it! We cannot be associated with a Booger-Eater!

JANE: Totally.

JANINE: I know, right?!

JANE: Well, what about that table.

JANINE: Oh yeah! I see Shelly over there. *(Waves)* Hey Shelly!!

JANE: *(Slaps her hand down)* Not Shelly! You have got to get over this whole "Shelly thing", which is doing absolutely nothing for us.

JANINE: What? I like Shelly. We used to watch cartoons when we were kids.

JANE: Word on the street is that she still likes to "watch cartoons", if you know what I mean.

JANINE: Oooooooooh... *(After thinking about it)* No, actually. I have no idea what that means.

Totally   *Joshua Evans*

JANE: Me neither. It's just what Kelsey told me.

(JANINE and JANE look at each other and shrug)

JANINE: What about those sophomore girls? My brother says that they're pretty cool.

JANE: *(Reluctantly)* Yeah… *(Convinced)* Yeah! So how should we handle this? Should we just go over there and sit down?

JANINE: Should we invite ourselves like that? Maybe we should introduce ourselves and then try to squeeze our way into some seats.

JANE: And after we sit down, they would totally be like, "Hey, you girls are pretty cool."

JANINE: "Ladies." We're in High School now. The proper term is "Ladies."

JANE: "Hey, you *ladies* are pretty cool."

JANINE: "You *ladies* should hang out with us every lunch."

JANE: "You ladies talk and dress totally cool."

JANINE: "You ladies *are* totally cool."

JANE: "We're heading out to the mall after school today; you ladies want to come with us?"

JANINE: "We're having a party on Saturday. You ladies down?"

JANE: "We're all going to State University when we graduate. You ladies totally have to apply."

JANINE: "I'm getting married, can you ladies be my Maids of Honor?"

Totally

(They look at each other and give a huge romantic sigh)

JANINE: Yeah. We should totally go over there.

JANE: I know, right?

(Beat)

JANINE: They do look pretty old.

JANE: I know, right?

(Beat)

JANINE: And lunch is pretty much half way over.

JANE: I know, right?

(Beat)

JANINE: Let's wait to make a move on them.

JANE: But not too long.

JANINE: Tomorrow?

JANE: Totally.

(The girls look around for a new place to sit. JANINE gets an idea)

JANINE: I know: *(Gestures to the right)* Right.

(JANINE and JANE exit)

BLACKOUT

"But tonight we ask the question: Was it bad luck, or was it some sort of ancient curse?"

Mysterious Mysteries

(Lights up on RICHARD. As he addresses the audience, dark "Mysterious Mysteries" TV music plays)

RICHARD: Good evening. Tonight's episode: The Curious Case of the Stuck Cowboys. Our story begins out west, with three cowboys, and their string of bad luck. But tonight we ask the question: Was it bad luck, or was it some sort of ancient curse? February 27, 1981. A cabin in the mountains of Colorado.

(Lights up on BILL, HAROLD, and MONTY)

BILL: We've been stuck in this here cabin for over four days.

HAROLD: I ain't never seen a snowstorm like this.

MONTY: Bill. Harold. If we don't find a way out of here soon, we're gonna starve.

BILL: Monty's right. I think we all know what we gotta do.

HAROLD: *(Nodding his head)* Decide who we're gonna eat first.

Mysterious Mysteries

MONTY: What? No. Jeeze, Harold. What's wrong with you?

BILL: Harold, your birthday's the worst.

(BILL, HAROLD, and MONTY freeze)

RICHARD: With no sign of the blizzard letting up, the three men seemed doomed. However, two days later, the three cowboys walked into the nearest town... 18 miles away. How did they do it? What happened in that cabin in the woods? No one truly knows. Some say they sold their souls to the devil.

(BILL puts on some devil horns. HAROLD and MONTY drop to their knees to beg)

HAROLD: Please, save us!

BILL: It'll cost ya.

MONTY: Sounds good!

(They freeze)

RICHARD: Some say they made a deal with the ghost of an Indian chief.

(HAROLD puts on an Indian headdress, as BILL removes his devil horns and joins MONTY to beg)

MONTY: Please save us!

HAROLD: It'll cost ya.

BILL: Sounds good!

(They freeze)

Mysterious Mysteries Joshua Evans

RICHARD: And even some say they were visited by a magical bear.

(MONTY puts on a bear head, as HAROLD removes his headdress and joins BILL to beg)

BILL: Please save us!

MONTY: Rooooooaaaarrrrrr!!!

HAROLD: Sounds good!

(They freeze)

RICHARD: Whatever the truth may be, their fate had been sealed. February 27, 1982. Exactly one year later.

(BILL, MONTY, and HAROLD stand and wait. An elevator bell chimes, and they step in)

BILL: *(Looking at the elevator buttons)* Is the lobby "M" or "1", I can never remember.

(The elevator comes to a screeching halt)

MONTY: No... nonononononono...

HAROLD: Stuck?! This can't be happening again!!

BILL: Stuck in a cabin, and now stuck in an elevator... Fellas, I think Harold's birthday's cursed!

MONTY: Why does this keep happening to us? What are we gonna do?!

HAROLD: We should definitely start brainstorming who we're gonna eat first.

Mysterious Mysteries

RICHARD: Although eventually rescued, their nightmare was just beginning. February 27, 1983.

(MONTY puts on a giant wig, as BILL sits in a chair, and HAROLD exits)

MONTY: *(As a woman)* No! You absolutely cannot go out and have a drink with your buddies.

BILL: But it's Harold's birthday. I'll only be gone for an hour.

MONTY: You don't love me, and you think I'm fat!

BILL: What are you talking about? I don't think you're fat.

MONTY: So now I'm a liar?!

BILL: What is happening? Look, darlin', maybe we should just take a break from each other.

MONTY: We can't! If you ever leave me, I don't know what I'll do! I'll throw myself from the tallest building! Besides, I think I might be pregnant! But I have no proof. You just have to believe me.

BILL: *(Completely exasperated)* Ugh!!! Darling!!! I... Wait... what's the date today? Is it February 27th?!!

MONTY: Who cares?!

BILL: *(With sudden realization, and utter terror)* I'm **stuck**...! In a bad relationship!

RICHARD: February 27th, 1984.

(HAROLD enters, wearing a different hat. MONTY removes his wig, as BILL exits)

Mysterious Mysteries   *Joshua Evans*

HAROLD: So, who do you know at this party?

MONTY: Oh, I know the birthday boy, Harold.

HAROLD: So, who are you voting for in this year's election?

MONTY: Oh, I don't like to talk about politics--

HAROLD: I'm Catholic, what's your religion?

MONTY: Um... I don't really think--

HAROLD: I see you're not married. Why not?

MONTY: Maybe I should go over--

(He tries to take a step away, but HAROLD sidesteps to cut him off from escaping)

HAROLD: Does this look infected to you?

MONTY: *(Gasps)* It's February 27th, isn't it?! I'm stuck! ...In an awkward conversation!

RICHARD: And who could forget 1985?

(MONTY exits, as HAROLD removes his hat. BILL enters, wearing a spider costume)

HAROLD: February 27th?

BILL: Yup.

HAROLD: Am I totally stuck in your web?

BILL: Yup.

Mysterious Mysteries

HAROLD: You gonna eat me?

BILL: Yup.

HAROLD: *Finally*, one of us gets eaten.

BILL: Happy Birthday.

> *("Mysterious Mysteries" music plays)*

RICHARD: How were these three men cursed? What did they do to deserve this annual anguish? And why was Harold so obsessed with one of them getting eaten? If you have any information, call our hotline at 1-800-MYSTERY.

BLACKOUT

*"Of course you're an evil terror. Terror **is** evil. It's like getting excited for a bread sandwich."*

SMILING UNICORN

(*Lights up on our hero, GIRL POW, tied to a chair, while the classic villain, EVILTERRA, feverishly works on a computer. JUMBA, our villain's dimwitted assistant, eagerly fidgets next to EVILTERRA*)

EVILTERRA: *(Spinning around to face GIRL POW and letting out a cackling, evil laugh)* Now nothing can stop me from destroying the sun, thanks to you, Girl Pow.

GIRL POW: You'll never get away with this, Evilterra!

EVILTERRA: But of course I will, Girl Pow. Now we both have front row seats as my Giant Lazer dooms this tiny planet. Girl Pow, you... "Girl Pow", what kind of stupid name is that? Girl Pow?

GIRL POW: Like yours is any better? Evilterra? Of course you're an evil terror. Terror *is* evil. It's like getting excited for a bread sandwich.

EVILTERRA: It's an *evil* name!

GIRL POW: It's a Scrabble Reject Word.

Smiling Unicorn

EVILTERRA: It's a family name!! *(Exasperated, she turns to JUMBA)* Jumba! Jumba? Jumba!! Bring down the Mega-Blade so we can slowly saw Girl Pow in half. *(JUMBA turns back towards the computers)* You see, Girl Pow, after I destroy the sun, I'm going to slowly cut you in half- *(JUMBA returns with the unplugged keyboard)* What are you doing?! Plug that back in! Without that, the Giant Lazer won't work, you fool! And bring down the Mega-Blade. *(JUMBA turns back)* Where was I?

GIRL POW: Slowly cutting me in half?

EVILTERRA: Yes! Thank you. We're going to slowly cut you- *(JUMBA taps her on the shoulder)* Jumba, I've told you not interrupt me when I'm monologu-ing. *(JUMBA offers her a butter knife)* What's this? *(JUMBA does a sawing motion)* We can't saw her in half with this! Where's the Mega-Blade? *(JUMBA makes a snapping motion)* It broke? *(JUMBA nods)* You broke it! *(JUMBA sheepishly offers the butter knife again)* You want me to saw her in half with a butter knife? *(JUMBA nods enthusiastically. EVILTERRA buries her face in her hands, and the doorbell rings)* Jumba, go get the door. *(JUMBA exits. EVILTERRA looks up to GIRL POW)* Good help is so hard to find.

MOM: *(From offstage)* Yoo-hoo!

EVILTERRA: Oh no...

(MOM, DAD, and SALLY enter with JUMBA)

MOM: Oh E, your new place it's... nice.

DAD: Looks like a cave.

MOM: Honey, be more supportive.

DAD: I **supported** her for six years in Villain School. And now she

Smiling Unicorn   *Joshua Evans*

lives in a cave.

EVILTERRA: *(Deadpan)* Mom. Dad. How great to see you.

SALLY: *(Playing with the computer with JUMBA trying to stop her)* Does this have any games?

EVILTERRA: Don't touch that, Sally, it's set perfectly to destroy the sun! Mom!

MOM: *(To EVILTERRA)* Don't yell at your little sister like that.

SALLY: Yeah, don't yell at me like that! *(Pointing to JUMBA)* Who's this?

MOM: Jumba! How good to see you. How are your mom and dad? *(JUMBA makes a "dead" motion)* Oh, I'm so sorry to hear that. How did they pass? *(JUMBA beams and points at himself, very proud)* Oh my.

DAD: I always warned George about you. *(To EVILTERRA, sarcastically)* Good to see you've improved the friends you hang out with.

GIRL POW: **Ah-hem!**

SALLY: Who's *that* weirdo?

GIRL POW: I'm Girl Pow!

DAD: Girl Pow? What is it with kid's names today? Idiot parents calling their kids Pineapple, Top Hat, Blarney Stone...

GIRL POW: You named your kid Evilterra!

MOM: That is a beautiful name. Besides, you're pronouncing it

Smiling Unicorn

wrong. It's "***Evul**-terra*". It's a traditional Scandinavian name, meaning "Smiling Unicorn".

GIRL POW: *(To EVILTERRA)* "Smiling Unicorn"? Your name, ***Evul**-terra*, literally translates to "Smiling Unicorn"? HA!

EVILTERRA: Mom. Dad. Can I see you in the corner, please?

(In a controlled rage, EVILTERRA quickly ushers MOM and DAD over to the corner. As she does, SALLY, JUMBA, and GIRL POW begin to play with GIRL POW's restraints. *See Notes*)

DAD: Smiling Unicorn is a glorious name to have.

EVILTERRA: That's not the point.

MOM: I'm confused, dear, what is the point?

EVILTERRA: The point is, is that you can't keep dropping in on my secret lairs unannounced all the time.

DAD: Don't I pay the rent on this secret lair?

EVILTERRA: That's just a loan.

DAD: A monthly recurring loan!

EVILTERRRA: Dad, I'm going to pay you and Mom back.

MOM: It's okay, honey Your father and I both know that you don't make a lot of money with this villain job. You'll pay us back when you can.

EVILTERRA: What did you say?

DAD: *(A little louder)* We pay your rent.

Smiling Unicorn   *Joshua Evans*

EVILTERRA: No, what did *you* say, Mom?

MOM: I said that we know that you don't make a lot of money with this villain job.

EVILTERRA: *(Seething mad)* Villain job?

DAD: Fine... Villain Mastermind or whatever silly title is printed on that villain diploma of yours.

EVILTERRA: It's not a "villain job". This is my life. I am a villain. That's who I am! A villain!!!

DAD: When you were a little girl, you thought you were a pretty, pink puppy. How's that working out for you?

EVILTERRA: Aaaaaaarrrrrgh!

SALLY: I didn't do it. I'll be in the car.

EVILTERRA: Car! Yes! Good! Good idea. All of you should go. *(She begins shooing MOM and DAD after SALLY and out the door)* Thank you for coming. Calling ahead next time would be wonderful. Goodbye. Farewell. Adios!

(EVILTERRA shoves them offstage and lets out a huge sigh. She composes herself, and turns around to face GIRL POW. All she sees is JUMBA, sitting in the chair tied up. JUMBA sheepishly smiles widely)

EVILTERRA: Jumbaaaaaa!

BLACKOUT

Stage directions behind EVILTERRA's back
SALLY has begun to poke at GIRL POW. JUMBA has taken a liking

Smiling Unicorn

to SALLY, and is copying her. As the scene in the corner continues, SALLY finds the end of the rope and starts pestering GIRL POW in the face with it. JUMBA thinks it's a game, takes it away from SALLY, and starts to pester SALLY in the face. SALLY takes it back and starts to run away from JUMBA, which is in a circle around GIRL POW. JUMBA pursues, until GIRL POW has been completely unraveled from the chair. Once free, GIRL POW stands. SALLY is dumbfounded by the newly freed GIRL POW. JUMBA is totally oblivious, and yanks the rope out of SALLY's hand, ecstatic that he has won his prize. With his eyes closed, she holds it close to his face, like a little girl and her doll. GIRL POW seizes the opportunity and sneaks up behind JUMBA and knocks him out. GIRL POW catches him before he falls to the ground, and spins him around back towards the chair, thus typing up JUMBA. GIRL POW sits JUMBA down in the chair. GIRL POW leaps to the computer, steals the keyboard, and quietly exits. SALLY exits saying, "I didn't do it. I'll be in the car."

"Brad... I want a bunny."

SURVIVAL: DANGER ISLAND [2039]

(Lights up on the Red Team, TED & SUE, the Purple Team, JOE & JANE, and BRAD & BECKY sitting on the floor. TED and SUE are dressed to suggests farmers, while JOE and JANE's outfits suggest military. RYAN, our television show's host, is standing, addressing the audience)

RYAN: Welcome back to Luxford Beach. On this season of Survival, our contestants have been forced to live and survive here on Danger Island. We've already seen the tribe vote off many strong teams, and tonight's Council is sure to be explosive.

JOE: *(Jumping to his feet)* Explosives?! Where?!

JANE: *(Joining him)* Everyone get down and cover! *(She rushes over to grab RYAN)*

RYAN: No, no, no... Joe. Jane. Relax.

Survival: Danger Island [2039]

TED: Whooooo-eee! We gonna see some explosions here tonight?

SUE: Hot dog! I love me some fireworks!!

RYAN: No, no... NO!! *(This silences the chaos)* Everyone sit down.

(Everyone sits back down)

RYAN: As I was saying, tonight's Council Meeting is sure to be ***exciting***. Our three remaining teams have battled hard, but one of the teams must leave the island tonight. Red Team, Purple Team: you've both chosen to let the other team speak first, so that leaves me with you two... *(turns to BRAD & BECKY)*

BRAD: *(Always smacking and chewing his gum)* 'Sup, Ryan.

RYAN: Brad. Becky. Who do you vote to leave Danger Island?

BECKY: *(Holding her phone up)* Does anyone else have service yet?

BRAD: 'Sup, Babe?

BECKY: I want service.

BRAD: Ok Babe. *(Turns to RYAN)* Hey Ryan. Ryan. You got any service here?

RYAN: No, Brad. We're on an island, secluded from the rest of the world. There is no use for cellular phones out here.

BRAD: Ok. *(Turns to BECKY)* Hey Babe. *(She looks up at him)* No service.

BECKY: *(Big sigh)* Whatever.

Survival: Danger Island [2039]   *Joshua Evans*

JOE: *(Jumping to his feet and saluting)* Ryan, Sir! Jane and I have changed our mind.

JANE: *(Also jumping to her feet)* Affirmative, Sir. We wish to vote now, not later.

RYAN: Guys, there's no need to salute me. Who would you like to vote off?

JOE: After much deliberation, we find it necessary to vote off Brad and Becky, Sir!

JANE: They never listen, and I might punch Brad in the face if he keeps eating his gum like that, Sir!

RYAN: I see. Well, that's two votes for Brad and Becky. Ted and Sue?

TED: Yeah, those two are slippery'er than a couple of crawfish in Jue-lie. I vote them.

SUE: I don't even think they know they're on a game show, Ryan.

RYAN: *(Turning to BRAD & BECKY)* That's four votes against you, Brad and Becky. I'm afraid the Island has Spoken. It's time to leave Danger Island.

BRAD: Ok cool.

(No one moves)

RYAN: So you have to leave now.

BECKY: *(Big sigh)* Fine.

(No one moves)

Survival: Danger Island [2039]

JANE: It has come to my attention that they are not removing themselves from the island, Sir.

JOE: Would you like for us to physically remove them, Sir?

JANE: Or we can officially challenge them to a push-up competition!

JOE: Push-Up Competition: GO!

(They both drop down and start vigorously doing push-ups)

RYAN: No, no. Relax guys. Brad, Becky... you have to leave.

BRAD: Yeah. Sounds good.

BECKY: Okay.

(No one moves)

TED: ...feel like we've been dropped off in the Twilight Zone.

SUE: Oh cow poop! Ted, are we in the Twilight Zone?

TED: Hey, Ryan? Is this TV show "The Twilight Zone"?

SUE: Ryan, I don't wanna be in no "Twilight Zone".

RYAN: It's not "The Twilight Zone"! *(Snapping his fingers in the face of BRAD and BECKY)* Guys! You have to leave! ...Guys!

BECKY: *(To BRAD)* Brad... I want a bunny.

BRAD: Sup, Babe?

BECKY: I want a bun-bunny.

Survival: Danger Island [2039]   *Joshua Evans*

BRAD: Cool, Babe. *(To RYAN)* Hey Ryan. You got a bunny?

RYAN: What?

BRAD: You got a bunny? Becky wants a bunny.

RYAN: There are no bunnies! *(Deep breath, then)* You. Two. Must. Leave.

BRAD: We gotta leave?

TED, SUE, JOE, JANE: Yes!

BRAD: Oh. My bad. *(Turns to BECKY)* Hey Babe?

BECKY: Did you get the bunny?

BRAD: No bunny, Babe. We gotta leave.

BECKY: *(Shrugs shoulders)* Okay.

RYAN: *(Addressing audience)* Brad and Becky have been voted off the island--

BECKY: *(To all the other contestants)* Have you got a bunny? I'm looking for a bunny. I heard there's a bunny somewhere around here. *(Etc)*

BRAD: *(At the same time, to all the other contestants)* Hey. Got a bunny? Bunny? Little rabbit? Huh? Anybody? Bunny? No? No? *(Etc)*

(BECKY and BRAD finally leave)

RYAN: Now only two teams remain. Four competitors will be tested by all that the island can throw at them. Ted, Sue. Joe, Jane.

Survival: Danger Island [2039]

You've made it this far in the competition--

(He's interrupted by the return of BRAD and BECKY. They are each carrying several stuffed bunnies)

BECKY: We found some bunnies. Do you guys, like, want some...?

BRAD: Bunnies. Bunnies for everyone. Yeah.

JOE: This is some kind of sick psychological warfare!

JANE: Abort! Abort! Abort!

(JOE and JANE run off)

BECKY: Is'cool. Is'like... more bunnies for us.

TED: This don't make no sense at all!

SUE: We *is* in the Twilight Zone! Our people never do well in the Twilight Zone!

(TED and SUE run off. Silence)

BRAD: Hey Ryan. *(RYAN refuses to look)* Hey Ryan. *(Still nothing)* Ryan. Ryan. Ryan. Hey Ryan.

RYAN: *(Spins to face him)* What Brad?! What do you want, Brad?!

BRAD: I think we won, Ryan.

RYAN: *(Storming off)* I quit. I'm not doing this with these two idiots.

(Silence)

Survival: Danger Island [2039] *Joshua Evans*

BRAD: Hey babe. *(BECKY looks up)* We won.

BECKY: Where did all these bunnies come from?

BRAD: Dunno. *(Pause)* Weird, huh?

BLACKOUT

"Um… hello? Girl from the future here. I might know a few things."

*C*ANNON AND *R*ADFORD

(Lights up on two Medieval lords, LORD CANNON and LORD RADFORD, dressed in battle gear, facing each other)

LORD CANNON: Well, well, well… if it isn't Lord Radford, and his ragtag little army.

LORD RADFORD: Lord Cannon, I thought I smelled you. Prepare to die.

LORD CANNON: With that puny excuse for an army? Most of them are farmers.

LORD RADFORD: So they know a pig when they see one.

LORD CANNON: Radford, yield this battlefield to me, and walk away with your head still attached.

LORD RADFORD: Cannon, your cruelty ends today.

(LACEY crashes onto the stage)

Cannon and Radford

LACEY: Woah! Awesome! *(She whips out her phone and starts texting)* OMG... you were totally right. LOL. *(She looks up at the two Lords)* Oh, hey guys, what's up?

LORD CANNON: I say, who are you?

LORD RADFORD: Yes, and what are you doing here?

LACEY: I'm Lacey. *(Pulls out some gum)* Want some gum?

LORD CANNON: Wench, you are lost.

LACEY: I am?

LORD RADFORD: Yes, Cannon is right. This is no place for a lady.

LACEY: Cannon? Lord Cannon? Then you gotta be Lord Radford, right?

LORD RADFORD: Are you one of my serfs?

LACEY: I have no idea what that means, but I know that I'm definitely in the right place. This is the big battle between Cannon and Radford!

LORD CANNON: But state your purpose here.

LACEY: *(She whips out a pad of paper and pencil)* What year is this?

LORD RADFORD: It is the year 1349 of our Lord.

LACEY: *(Writing it down)* 134*9*! I was *so* gonna say that! I knew that it was either 1349 or 1397! Great. Thanks guys!

Cannon and Radford *Joshua Evans*

LORD CANNON: This whelp doesn't know what year it is!

LACEY: Oh, I'm not from this time. I'm actually in 3rd period World History, and we have a big test today.

LORD RADFORD: 3rd period, World History?

LACEY: Yeah. Teacher is pretty cool, and he lets us use one Time Travel per test. I completely blanked on when you two fought each other, so I used my Time Travel on you guys.

LORD CANNON: I don't understand, what do you mean "time travel"?

LACEY: It's cool, you don't have to understand. It's way beyond your noggin. *(Noticing somebody offstage)* Hey, there's Kelly. *(Waving)* Hey Kelly! You couldn't nail these questions either? Ha! I **told** you we should've studied this chapter more! Text me later!

LORD RADFORD: M'lady, I'm afraid that you have to leave now. This ogre and I have unfinished business.

LACEY: Dude. You're totally right. Gotta jet. *(Starts to leave, then stops)* Hey, you guys are army dudes. What was the name of the guy who originally conquered this land?

LORD CANNON: That was my great, great grandfather: Blar the Cruel.

LACEY: Blar! How could I forget such a stupid name?! Thanks, I gotta go change that answer.

LORD CANNON: His name is not stupid!

LACEY: "Blar"? Whatever dude, get over it. Was he really your great, great grandfather? I wonder if I could snag some extra credit

Cannon and Radford

for that little nugget.

LORD RADFORD: M'lady, please…

LACEY: Say no more, it's *time* I was going. *(Trying to make a joke)* He, he, he… "time".

LORD CANNON: Go!

LACEY: Woah, relax dude. *(She starts to leave, then stops)* Oh, BTW… which one of you was Cannon again?

LORD CANNON: *(Puffs out his chest)* I am the great Lord Cannon.

LACEY: Yeah, you might wanna go home.

LORD CANNON: Ha! Why is that?!

LACEY: *(Pointing to herself)* Um… hello? Girl from the future here. I might know a few things.

LORD CANNON: Don't be absurd.

LACEY: Seriously, your neck and those farmers: not a good combo for you.

LORD CANNON: *(Pointing to LORD RADFORD's army)* Ha! **Those** farmers?

LACEY: *(Mocking him)* Ha! And **those** pitchforks.

LORD CANNON: I will not be cowed by peasants!

LACEY: Whatever, man. *(She high-fives LORD RADFORD)* Radford, you got this. *(She gives LORD CANNON a menacing decapitating motion. Then smiles)* See ya' guys!

Cannon and Radford   *Joshua Evans*

(LACEY exits)

LORD CANNON: Good riddance. Now, where were we?

LORD RADFORD: And you still want to go through with this?

(KELLY walks over)

KELLY: Hey, what's up guys?

LORD CANNON: *(Exploding)* It's 1349!

KELLY: I'm just looking for Lacy.

LORD RADFORD: She left.

KELLY: Cool, thanks. Which one of you is Cannon? *(LORD CANNON growls at her)* Ah… well… good luck, buddy.

(KELLY exits)

LORD RADFORD: *(Beaming)* Well… I'm all set. You?

BLACKOUT

"Casey, you're a 35 year old toddler."

Time Reporting

(Lights up on DIRK, LINDA, and CASEY, three news anchors sitting at a news desk. CASEY is playing air drums with two pencils as drumsticks)

DIRK: Welcome back to Channel 5 Action News. I'm Dirk Thunderman.

LINDA: And I'm Linda Powerstreet.

CASEY: And Iiiiiiiii'm Casey.

DIRK: Yes, we'd like to *once again* introduce our new co-host, Casey Worthington.

CASEY: Iiiiiiii'm Casey.

LINDA: You don't need to repeat that, every time we come back from a commercial.

CASEY: My dad owns the building!

Time Reporting

DIRK: *(Sighs, but stays professional)* He sure does, Casey. He sure does.

CASEY: Casey Time!

LINDA: Returning to our top story this evening: Channel 5 Action News is debuting our amazing new technology, Time Reporting.

DIRK: Using Quantum Mirroring, we're able to look backwards or forwards through time on this day, April 14th.

CASEY: Mirrors confuse me. How does my reflection know what I'm going to do?

LINDA: Casey, you're a 35 year old toddler.

CASEY: Casey Time!

DIRK: Using the Time Reporting, we take you back to April 14th, 10,000 years ago. And to our man on the scene, Gronk.

(Lights shift to GRONK, a caveman, who is oblivious to our news anchors at first)

LINDA: Gronk? Gronk, can you hear us?

(GRONK looks around above his head, trying to figure out where the voice is coming from)

GRONK: Gronk?

LINDA: Yes, Gronk, thank you for joining us. What can you tell us about your life there?

GRONK: Gronk!

Time Reporting *Joshua Evans*

LINDA: I see. And what about your views on the coming Ice Age?

GRONK: *("Not too bad")* Gronk.

LINDA: Thank you, Gronk. We'll check back in with you in a bit.

GRONK: *(Big thumbs up, and yells to the sky)* Gronk!

(Lights fade on GRONK)

LINDA: Fascinating stuff. What do you think, Casey?

CASEY: *(He's playing with a lighter)* I found a lighter!

DIRK: *(Looking at the "camera")* What idiot gave him that?

CASEY: I just find stuff!

DIRK: *(Sighs)* Let's take you live to April 14th, 1912. I understand our field reporter, Charlotte, is on board the maiden voyage of--

(Lights shift to reveal CHARLOTTE, dressed for a party, with a martini glass in hand)

CHARLOTTE: A big ol' boat, Dirk! And it's huge! It's so big, it's called the Titanic. Do you know how to spell Titanic, Dirk? P-A-R-T-Y!

LINDA: Charlotte, I hate to tell you this, but your ship--

CHARLOTTE: *(Sings to the tune of Tupac Shakur's "California")* Big Titanic, knows how to party. Big Titanic, knows how to paaaartayy. In the sea, the north sea. In the sea, Atlantic--

DIRK: No, Charlotte. Your ship will sink tonight.

Time Reporting

CHARLOTTE: You know it, Dirk! It's going down tonight!

LINDA: Charlotte. Listen: it's going down... for real.

CHARLOTTE: *(Singing)* It's going down for real!

(Lights fade on CHARLOTTE)

DIRK: Well, at least she's having a good time. *(Looking at Casey)* Is that a knife?

CASEY: *(He's now playing with a lighter and a knife)* Flaming knife!

LINDA: *(To camera)* Feel free to call Security at any time.

CASEY: *(To himself)* Flaming knife... of Dooooooom.

LINDA: *(Takes a pause)* We now take you live to... *(checks his earpiece)* do I have this right...? Thirty minutes into the future... here at the news station?

(Lights shift to reveal FUTURE DIRK. He wears tattered and torn versions of DIRK'S clothing)

FUTURE DIRK: Dirk! It's me, Dirk.

DIRK: Excuse me?

FUTURE DIRK: No, excuse *us.*

DIRK: You're me.

FUTURE DIRK: And I'm you.

DIRK: And we're we?

Time Reporting *Joshua Evans*

FUTURE DIRK: *(Pointing at DIRK)* Dirk.

DIRK: *(Points back at FUTURE DIRK)* Dirk.

CASEY: Casey!

FUTURE DIRK: Caught up now?

DIRK: Clear as crystal.

FUTURE DIRK: *(Points at CASEY)* Kill him.

DIRK: Excuse us?

FUTURE DIRK: He single-handedly destroys the newsroom.

CASEY: *(Whispers)* Flaming Knife of Doom.

DIRK: I can't kill him.

FUTURE DIRK: Look at me. I woke up, right where you're sitting, and the entire building was burning around me.

DIRK: Fine. I'll take care of him.

FUTURE DIRK: Team Dirk!

(Lights fade on FUTURE DIRK)

DIRK: *(To CASEY, holding out his hand)* Lighter. *(CASEY hands him the lighter)* Knife. *(CASEY hands him the knife)* Now sit. *(CASEY sits on the floor)* No, on a chair, you idiot. *(CASEY does)* New game: see how long you can stare at the stage lights. Ready, go!

CASEY: *(Staring at the lights)* Ow.

Time Reporting

LINDA: Doing great, Mongo. Let's check back in with Gronk.

(Lights shift back to GRONK, who is holding a large branch)

GRONK: *(Pointing to branch)* Gronk.

LINDA: That's great, Gronk. And what do you use that branch for?

GRONK: *(Begins sweeping the floor with the branch)* Gronk. *(Scratches his back with it)* Gronk. *(Fans himself with it)* Gronk.

LINDA: What a wonderful invention. And what do you call it?

GRONK: *(Gronk looks at the branch, back at LINDA, back at the branch, and back at LINDA)* Gronk.

LINDA: Walked into that one, didn't I? Well Gronk, thank you for--

(As LINDA has been talking, a large bear is sneaking up on GRONK)

DIRK: Gronk! Watch out!!

(GRONK turns and the bear pounces on him. The two of them engage in a wrestling match, taking turns saying nothing but "Gronk!" and "Bear!". GRONK eventually wins the match)

DIRK: Well done, Gronk! We're so glad that you were able to win that battle.

GRONK: *(Looks down at the bear, then up at DIRK)* **Bare**-ly.

(GRONK erupts with laughter at his own joke, and walks off, chanting his name. Lights fade)

DIRK: I like that guy.

Time Reporting   *Joshua Evans*

CASEY: *(Holds up a trident)* I've got a trident!

LINDA: What?!

CASEY: I find things!

LINDA: Tridents?!

CASEY: Casey Time!

DIRK: I'm going to wrap this up as quickly as I can. Back to Charlotte...

(Lights up on CHARLOTTE)

CHARLOTTE: *(Singing)* Stayin' alive, stayin' alive. Ah, ha, ha, ha, stayin' alive, stayin' alive--

DIRK: Your irony knows no bounds, Charlotte.

CHARLOTTE: Dirk! You're just in time! The captain is letting the passengers take turns driving the boat.

LINDA: Listen to me... you really really really need to be careful of icebergs out there.

CHARLOTTE: *(Genuinely concerned)* Icebergs! Good heavens! *(Holds up martini glass)* We **were** running low on ice!

LINDA: No! In our time, you're on a very famous ship which will crash--

CHARLOTTE: *(She stops cold, and exclaims)* Famous?!! *(Begins singing)* FAME! I'm gonna live forever...

DIRK: Goodbye, Charlotte

Time Reporting

CHARLOTTE: Okay! Talk to you soon.

(Lights fade on CHARLOTTE)

DIRK: Let's wrap this up with one last look at 30 minutes into the future.

(Lights shift to reveal FUTURE DIRK)

FUTURE DIRK: *("What happened?")* Dirk!

DIRK: *("What did I do?")* Dirk.

FUTURE DIRK: I thought you were going to take care of this guy!

DIRK: I took away his stuff. He's literally just staring at the lights right now.

FUTURE DIRK: You doof!

DIRK: You're the doof!

LINDA: Technically, you're both doofs.

FUTURE DIRK & DIRK: Shut up, Linda.

FUTURE DIRK: Thirty minutes from now, a partially blinded Casey sets fire to the entire building.

DIRK: With what? I took away his lighter.

FUTURE DIRK: That idiot MacGyver always finds a way!

DIRK: Relax, Future Dirk! Or so help me, I will turn this timeline around.

Time Reporting   *Joshua Evans*

FUTURE DIRK: I'm totally relaxed! I'm Mr. Relaxed over here! I'm the mayor of Relax-Town!

DIRK: That's it mister, I'm gonna hold my breath until I pass out! That'll relax you!

(DIRK takes a big breath and holds it)

FUTURE DIRK: No, you dummy! Stop! I ***told you:*** I wake up and the station's destroyed! So don't pass yourself out! *(DIRK passes out)* Man!! I'm such an idiot!!

(FUTURE DIRK storms off)

LINDA: Thanks for watching Channel 5 Action News. Have a good night.

CASEY: *(Displaying a huge firework)* Cool! I found a firework!

LINDA: *(Jumps up)* For the love of...! Clear the building!

(LINDA runs off)

CASEY: Casey Time!

BLACKOUT

"My good man, you're slowing down the race of the century!"

The Commodore and The Admiral

(Lights up on a courtroom setting. The JUDGE, in his robe, is sitting at his desk. Suddenly, a huge group of people storm on stage. It is the COMMODORE and the ADMIRAL, followed closely by JARVIS and JEEVES. They are being pushed and shoved by an angry group of townsfolk. Among the townsfolk is the FARMER, the MARKET MAN, and the FERRYMAN. The COMMODORE and the ADMIRAL are each wearing top hats, monocles, and mustaches. JARVIS and JEEVES each wear a bow tie and tux jackets)

JUDGE: *(Yelling at everyone, controlling the room)* Excuse me! *(The room calms itself)* What is going on here?

COMMODORE: I assume you're some sort of authority here?

JUDGE: Yes, I am the Judge for this small town.

ADMIRAL: Excellent. Release us at once.

The Commodore and The Admiral

FARMER, MARKET MAN, FERRYMAN: No / This is an outrage / Arrest them immediately / etc.

JUDGE: Quiet! *(To the COMMODORE and the ADMIRAL)* First we must hear the complaints of the people, listen to what they have to say--

COMMODORE: *(Interrupting)* I'm sorry, but you bore me!

JUDGE: Excuse me?!

ADMIRAL: We're adrift in a sea of boredom.

JUDGE: Who are you?

COMMODORE: *(Cuing him)* Jarvis?

JARVIS: *(Announces regally)* May I present Commodore Billingsborough... the third.

ADMIRAL: *(Cuing him)* Jeeves.

JEEVES: *(Announcing regally)* And Admiral Rufustonsington... the fourth.

COMMODORE & ADMIRAL: *(Bowing)* Esquire.

FARMER: *(In tears)* They've completely ruined my life!

MARKET MAN: *(Wide eyed, and shaking)* They should be hung!

FERRYMAN: Judge hurt them!

JUDGE: Easy everyone. Commodore, Admiral... it looks like you've angered a few of my fellow townsfolk. Our law declares that we hear them out. Let's start with hearing your side of the story first.

The Commodore and The Admiral *Joshua Evans*

COMMODORE: My good man, you're slowing down the race of the century!

ADMIRAL: We're racing each other around the world... around the world, I say!!

COMMODORE: It all began three weeks ago, when we were enjoying a delightful afternoon at our Filthy Rich Social Club--

ADMIRAL: When a marvelous idea struck me. "Billingsborough," I said--

COMMODORE: "Yes, Rufustonsington?" I replied--

ADMIRAL: "Let us race each other around the world!"

COMMODORE: "A wonderful idea! And the wager?"

ADMIRAL: "A magoollian dollars!"

COMMODORE: "Brilliant!"

ADMIRAL: "Leave today?"

COMMODORE: "Smashing!"

ADMIRAL: Flash ahead three weeks, and this speck of a town has slowed our journey tremendously.

JUDGE: I see. Um... "a magoollian dollars"?

ADMIRAL: Quite right.

JUDGE: And just how much is a magoollian dollars?

COMMODORE: Why, it's a number only us Magoollianaires are

The Commodore and The Admiral

aware of.

JUDGE: Okay. *(Motions)* And these two?

ADMIRAL: These are our butlers. Professionals in every way. *(Looks at JARVIS & JEEVES)* Right?

JARVIS / JEEVES: Yes sir; Absolutely; No doubt about it; 110%

COMMODORE: Professional Yes-Men.

FARMER: They should be ashamed!

JUDGE: *(To the FARMER)* Anderson, what happened?

FARMER: *(Through tears)* They came from the sky! Bringing destruction!

ADMIRAL: Our hot air balloons... happened upon his farm.

FARMER: Two giant, flying rail cars! Crashed straight through my barn!

COMMODORE: Easily repairable.

FARMER: ...Landed on my prize cow!

ADMIRAL: Cushioned the landing.

FARMER: ...While my wife was milking her!

COMMODORE: Bad timing.

FARMER: ...With my favorite dog. *(Lowers his head to cry)*

JARVIS: The dirt poor farmer had never felt sorrow so intense...

The Commodore and The Admiral   _{Joshua Evans}

JEEVES: His inconsolable tears flowed like a river through the desert lines of his weathered face.

(The JUDGE, who is trying to comfort the FARMER, looks at the ADMIRAL inquisitively)

ADMIRAL: Professional Narrators.

COMMODORE: You can't have a race around the world without a good Narrator!

MARKET MAN: *(Wide-eyed with fear)* They destroyed our market street, Judge.

ADMIRAL: Well, that's a matter of opinion, really.

MARKET MAN: Matter of opinion?! They tore through our market street, riding elephants! I've never been so terrified in my life!

JUDGE: Elephants?!

MARKET MAN: Big, tall, gray animals. They have tusks and a trunk.

JUDGE: I know what an elephant is! *(To the COMMODORE)* Elephants?

COMMODORE: Our balloons were down, we had to ride ***something***.

MARKET MAN: Elephants, Judge!!! *(Under his breath, terrified)* Elephants!

JUDGE: *(Turns to the FERRYMAN)* Tug, what happened to you?

FERRYMAN: Tug work on docks. Tug run ferry boat. Tug good at

The Commodore and The Admiral

his work. Tug take personal pride in a job well done.

ADMIRAL: *(Letting out a huge exasperation noise)* My kingdom for a pronoun!

FERRYMAN: Tug pulling ferry boat across river. Ferry boat get closer. Through fog, Tug listen. Tug hear something Tug never hear before. Tug look out at river, and see *(pointing at the COMMODORE and the ADMIRAL)* thems two, with thems two *(indicating JARVIS and JEEVES)* playing strange music with these!

(TUG produces two strange instruments from a sack that he's been carrying. The JUDGE takes them)

JUDGE: What are these?

COMMODORE: Gwin-daddles. Only the filthy-rich know of them.

JUDGE: What are they for?

ADMIRAL: *(Snaps or claps)* Jarvis. Jeeves.

(JARVIS and JEEVES jump to attention, and take the instruments from TUG. They begin to "play" bizarre music. The COMMODORE and the ADMIRAL are extremely entertained, keeping the beat. The music stops)

ADMIRAL: *(To the JUDGE)* Professional Race Music.

JUDGE: I've heard enough. The evidence seems quite clear, and you two deny nothing. I'm going to have to lock you up until I can investigate further.

COMMODORE: *(Throwing down his hat)* Preposterous!

ADMIRAL: *(Throwing down his hat)* Absurd!

The Commodore and The Admiral   Joshua Evans

COMMODORE: The race must continue!!

JUDGE: Enough!!

ADMIRAL: Very well then. Jarvis? Jeeves?

(JARVIS and JEEVES bow their heads in acknowledgment. They suddenly burst into a loud, rambunctious, silly display of sound and movement with their "gwin-daddles". All eyes are transfixed on the strange performance, as the COMMODORE and the ADMIRAL slip away and escape unseen. JARVIS and JEEVES come to a dramatic conclusion, and hold their pose. A beat, then...)

JARVIS: Oh... Professional Getaway Distraction.

(Everyone turns, and is shocked to see that their prisoners have escaped. In an roar, they chase after them offstage. Once they're gone. JARVIS and JEEVES toss away their "gwin-daddles" and retrieve the top hats. They dust them off and put them on)

JEEVES: *(In a proper accent, similar to the ADMIRAL'S)* I say, Commodore. Are we done with this silly charade?

JARVIS: *(Also in a proper accent)* Quite right, quite right, Admiral.

JEEVES: We shall need to acquire two new servents.

JARVIS: A pity. Those two were so good.

JEEVES: Onwards with the race?!

JARVIS: Bully!

BLACKOUT

"This is, like, my first holographic test."

Final Exam

(Lights up as GERRY enters. MIRAGE comes to life)

MIRAGE: Activation. Today's date: 8th of March, 3045. Hello. My name is Mirage. I will be your personal android for this holographic test.

GERRY: Um... Hey Mirage. I'm Gerry. ...With a "G". This is, like, my first holographic test. Coach says I need to score a 85 or higher, or else I'm gonna lose my scholarship on the hyper-ball team. Like, I really really need this.

MIRAGE: I understand, Gerry with a "G". You are dumb, and need a good grade. Is this correct?

GERRY: Um... Yeah.

MIRAGE: Very well, Gerry with a "G". Let's begin. This test is for your class: 21st Century Holidays. Is this correct?

GERRY: The weird-American-holidays-class... yeah.

Final Exam

MIRAGE: Very well. I will ask you questions, and the following holograms will assist. Answer too many questions incorrectly, and we enter a Sudden Death Lightning Round.

GERRY: That sounds scary.

MIRAGE: It's very stressful.

(They walk towards the first hologram)

MIRAGE: Question One. Please identify the proper subtext for the following Thanksgiving statement:

(The holographic DAD comes to life)

DAD: Hello George and Shelia, my wife's parents. Oh, you've decided to stay for the whole weekend? Wonderful. That makes me very pleased, and I cannot wait to create new memories with you.

GERRY: Oh man. Tough one.

MIRAGE: Is the proper subtext A:

DAD: *(Through gritted teeth)* Hello George and Shelia, my wife's parents. That sure is a lot of bags for one night. Isn't this going to be fun. Megan, my wife, can I speak to you privately, please?

MIRAGE: ...B:

DAD: *(Over the top)* George and Shelia! Still alive, huh?! Staying for the whole weekend? Excellent! I'll be hiding in the garage, but please feel free to stop by and punch my pride as soon as you get settled in.

MIRAGE: ...or C:

Final Exam   *Joshua Evans*

(DAD lets out a huge, long scream)

GERRY: Um... "C"?

MIRAGE: Incorrect. The answer is "D: All of the Above."

GERRY: Bummer-sauce.

MIRAGE: Question Two. Fill in the blank. In the year 2152, President Morris made this statement:

(PRESIDENT MORRIS comes to life)

PRESIDENT MORRIS: And so, my fellow Americans, it is with great honor, joy, and triumph that I declare this day to be a new national holiday. Today we officially celebrate National....

(PRESIDENT MORRIS freezes, mid-sentence)

GERRY: Dang. This is hard. Um... National Big Gulp Day.

MIRAGE: Incorrect. The answer is:

(PRESIDENT MORRIS comes to life)

PRESIDENT MORRIS: Today we officially celebrate National Super Bowl Day.

GERRY: It used to be only *one* day?! Whoa.

MIRAGE: Keep up, Gerry with a "G". Question Three. Which of these terrifyingly absurd, and ludicrous mascots was **not** a mascot of a 21st Century holiday?

(MASCOT 1 comes to life)

Final Exam

MASCOT 1: *(Extremely creepy)* Hello child. Sleep now. Let your dreams take you away. For when you sleep, I shall enter your home, eat your food, and leave suspicious packages for you to wonder about. All year long, you had better be good, or I shall leave combustables in your sock. Hohohohohohoho... to all a good night.

(MASCOT 2 comes to life)

MASCOT 2: Psssst! Hey! Hey Kid! You like fire? Huh?! Yeah... you like fire, don't you? You like to blow things up? You like to watch things burn? You wanna set the whole world on fire?! You do, don't ya?! It's okay!!! *(Uncle Sam -like)* I want you... to light this on fire.

(MASCOT 3 comes to life)

MASCOT 3: *(Long beat)* I'm a six foot bunny. I'm a mammal, yet I lay eggs. Weeeeeeird colored eggs. Here's a chocolate depiction of me. Eat it. *(Beat)* Peeps.

GERRY: Whoa.

MIRAGE: Indeed.

GERRY: That's just weird, dude.

MIRAGE: Very weird, "dude".

GERRY: Ummmmmm... Number 3?

MIRAGE: Incorrect. The answer is D: None of the Above.

GERRY: Again?! Why don't you tell me that "D" is an option?!

MIRAGE: *(Makes an alarm sound)* Warning! Warning! You are running out of questions, and you have not answered a single one

Final Exam *Joshua Evans*

correct. According to my calculations, you need to answer all remaining questions correctly in order to pass.

GERRY: Lightning Round?

MIRAGE: Lightning Round.

(All holograms reorganize themselves, and come to life one at a time)

MIRAGE: Identify each holiday correctly, or face elimination. Are you ready, Gerry with a "G"?

GERRY: Hit me.

(DAD): *(Massive amount of crying)* Nobody loves me! I can't get a girlfriend to save my life! Construction paper and doilies are tear-stained and strewn across my bedroom floor!

GERRY: Valentine's Day!

MIRAGE: Correct.

(PRESIDENT MORRIS): *(Severly sarcastic)* No no no! PLEASE take all my money! What could I *possibly* use that money for?! What's that you say...? You've been taking money out of my paycheck all year? Well, why stop there?! Let me give you MORE!!

GERRY: Tax Day!

MIRAGE: Correct.

(MASCOT 1): Hey! Gimme all you got! Put it in the bag! Don't you hold back on me... Gimme that. And that! And that too! A pencil?! You think I want a pencil?! Gimme another peanut butter cup! You better HOPE I don't come back here with my little brother.

Final Exam

GERRY: Halloween!

MIRAGE: Correct.

(MASCOT 2): (Five!) Last year? Pff! Last year don't mean a thing. (Four!) THIS.. *this* is my year. (Three!) Exercise, eating right, gonna write that novel... (Two!) Waitwaitwaitwaitwait... we're already at "two"? (One!) One?! I gotta find someone to kiss! Anyone?! Anyone?! (Happy New Year!!) ...great. Another year alone.

GERRY: New Year's Eve!

MIRAGE: Correct.

(MASCOT 3): Why don't you call? You never call! You don't love me. Whatever happened to what's-her-name? I've got a weird bunion on my toe, do you think it's serious? Mrs. Cutherbert's son just graduated from medical school; how's your online degree going? Yes, I paid your rent this month.

GERRY: Mother's Day!

MIRAGE: Correct. Congratulations. You have passed.

GERRY: YES!!

MIRAGE: How will you celebrate?

GERRY: I'm going to Disneyland!

MIRAGE: I'm sorry it's closed today.

GERRY: It is?

MIRAGE: Yes, in remembrance of National Book Day.

Final Exam

GERRY: Oh yeah. *(Beat)* Books. That must've been weird. *(Beat)* Can you John Hughes me out?

MIRAGE: Of course, Gerry.

("Don't You [Forget About Me]" plays as the whole group does the classic fist-pump-to-the-heavens pose. GERRY is pleased and walks out, as everyone else is frozen as the music swells)

GERRY: Cool.

BLACKOUT

"Boo-yeah! I'm hungry. I wish for a twinkie."

Cindy's Best Day Ever

(Lights up on CINDY as she walks on stage. She is singing a song about how cool she is. She notices a lamp on the floor. She picks it up)

CINDY: Whoa... cool. I wonder...

(She rubs the lamp. GENIE enters)

GENIE: I am the Genie of the lamp!

CINDY: Aw yeeah!

GENIE: Who has summoned me?

CINDY: Me! Cindy! Me! Down here!

GENIE: Cindy, I shall grant you three wishes.

CINDY: Boo-yeah! I'm hungry. I wish for a twinkie.

GENIE: Granted!

Cindy's Best Day Ever

(GENIE tosses her a twinkie. CINDY puts the twinkie in her pocket)

CINDY: Twinkie for me! Yo, Genie! Seond wish: you now my all-time Twinkie Genie.

GENIE: Granted!

CINDY: Only three wishes?

GENIE: Correct, Cindy.

CINDY: Gotcha. Last wish: I wish for infinite wishes.

GENIE: Grant-- Wait... What?

CINDY: Gimme gimme gimme wishes in my chimmney.

GENIE: That... that's not a saying.

CINDY: I hear you talking, but I'm not seeing infinite wishes.

GENIE: Wishing for more wishes is against the rules.

CINDY: Rules are made for chumps.

GENIE: I cannot grant you infinite wishes.

CINDY: Fine then... I wish for your Genie Twin.

GENIE: Granted! ...wait, what?

CINDY: Too late!

(GENIE II enters)

GENIE II: I am the Genie of the lamp!

Cindy's Best Day Ever *Joshua Evans*

CINDY: Awesome!

GENIE: This isn't right.

GENIE II: Who has summoned me?

CINDY: Me! Cindy! Me! Down here!

GENIE: Don't listen to her.

GENIE II: I shall grant you three wishes.

CINDY: Bam to the wham!

GENIE: This is cheating.

GENIE II: Quiet Twinkie Genie.

CINDY: Ha! He called you Twinkie Genie!

GENIE: I'm out of here.

CINDY: Ah ah ah! You gotta stay. You my all-time Twinkie Genie.

GENIE II: That was dumb to let her do that to you.

CINDY: Yup. But you about to T-Ripple Dumb her.

GENIE II: T-Ripple Dumb?

CINDY: Yeah: Triple Dumb. *(Singing)* Dumb, dumb, dummmmmmb!

GENIE II: That's... that's not what that means...

CINDY: I wish for another me!

Cindy's Best Day Ever

GENIE: Don't do it!

GENIE II: I have no choice!

CINDY: *(Singing)* Dumb, dumb, dummmmmmb!

GENIE II: Granted!

(CINDY II enters, and joins CINDY)

CINDY II: What up?!

CINDY: Oooooo! You look good!

CINDY II: Learned from the best...

CINDY / CINDY II: ...us!

GENIE: This is ridiculous.

GENIE II: Can this get any worse?

CINDY: I shall call you CD...

CINDY II: Cindy Dos?

CINDY: Mm-hm!

CINDY II: And I shall call you OC...

CINDY: Original Cindy?

CINDY II: *(She puts up a fist bump)* Hit it!

(CINDY and CINDY II fist bump, and blow it up. They knock themselves to the ground. The genies let out an exasperated groan)

Cindy's Best Day Ever   *Joshua Evans*

CINDY: Twinkie?

CINDY II: You know me too well.

CINDY: Twinkie Genie! Hit me!

GENIE: I refuse.

(CINDY and CINDY II gasp)

CINDY II: He can't do that. *(To GENIE)* You can't do that!

CINDY: CD, gimme one of your wishes, so I can show him who's boss.

CINDY II: Hey! T-Ripple! Give her one of my wishes.

GENIE II: Granted!

CINDY: Boom! Now you in trouble, Twinkie Genie!

GENIE: Uh oh... You better make sure I learn my lesson...

CINDY: Oh, I will.

GENIE II: ...And punish us Genies pretty good...

CINDY II: Oh... it's coming.

GENIE: Oh no please... don't wish for all of us to all go away and get you all the Twinkies in the whole wide world.

CINDY: That's *exactly* what I'm gonna wish for.

GENIE II: Oh no...

Cindy's Best Day Ever

CINDY: I wish for you all to go away--

GENIE: Granted!

CINDY: What?

GENIE: You wish for us all to go away.

CINDY: But you didn't let me finish my sentence!

GENIE II: No take-backs!

GENIE: Bye!

(GENIE "poofs" and exits)

GENIE II: Bye!

(GENIE II "poofs" exits)

CINDY II: *(Getting sucked offstage)* Stay cool! Be the best Cindy ev-ah!

(Beat. CINDY looks around)

CINDY: Ha. Joke's on them... *(Pulls out her Twinkie)* Free Twinkie.

BLACKOUT

INDEX

Two(ish) Actors

Marion vs. Marion	26
Sandwich	62
Totally	84

Three(ish) Actors

Cannon and Radford	114
Ryan's Fans	10

Four Actors

Atlantis!	56
Cindy's Best Day Ever	146
Mysterious Mysteries	90
Philophobia	2
Trapped	42

Five Actors

Isla Peligroso – 1839	68
Kitchen Floor	48
So You Think You Can News	32

Six Actors

Smiling Unicorn	98
Time Reporting	120
The Garden	16

Seven Actors

Final Exam	138
Survival: Danger Island [2039]	106

Eight Actors

A Saturday Afternoon	76
The Commodore and The Admiral	130

The Author and the Illustrator

Joshua Evans

Originally from the Pacific Northwest region, Joshua is a proud graduate of Washington State University where he earned a BA in Theatre Arts. Currently residing in Los Angeles with his wife and baby boy, he spends most of his time staring out the window, missing the rain. Joshua has appeared in a handful of television shows, as well as numerous stage productions in La-La Land. Along with his acting credits, he has written/directed/acted in three short films thru his company, Skewed Evans Productions (www.skewedevansproductions.com). Meanwhile, in his non-acting world, Joshua lists among his highlights and accomplishments the following: been arrested in India, was hogtied to railroad tracks and left for dead, snuck into a Kanye music video in Prague, eaten scorpion, been punched in the face, camped in a Bedouin tent outside of Petra, been kicked off a train, broken up a fight between Michael Strahan and two dwarfs, crashed a moped on Easter Island, hates bread, and is terrified of aliens.

Sean Hall

Sean was born a poor southern kid in a rural Montana hospital, which has since burned down. (He was later acquitted on all charges.) After landing his dream job at 19 by being hired to dress up in a draft horse costume and dancing in front of strangers, its all been downhill from there. Four college degrees, one high school sweetheart and a gastric bypass surgery later, he is currently attempting to set the sequential art world on fire. This book is one of his first attempts to start the kindling.